THE HANDMAID'S TALE

Margaret Atwood

EDITORIAL DIRECTOR Justin Kestler
EXECUTIVE EDITOR Ben Florman
DIRECTOR OF TECHNOLOGY Tammy Hepps

SERIES EDITORS John Crowther, Justin Kestler
MANAGING EDITOR Vince Janoski

WRITERS Ross Douthat, Selena Ward
EDITORS Sarah Friedberg, Emma Chastain

This edition published by Spark Publishing

Spark Publishing
A Division of SparkNotes LLC
120 Fifth Avenue, 8th Floor
New York, NY 10011

Please submit all comments and questions or report errors to www.sparknotes.com/errors

Printed and bound in the United States

ISBN 1-58663-517-4

Introduction:
Stopping to Buy Sparknotes on a Snowy Evening

Whose words these are you *think* you know.
Your paper's due tomorrow, though;
We're glad to see you stopping here
To get some help before you go.

Lost your course? You'll find it here.
Face tests and essays without fear.
Between the words, good grades at stake:
Get great results throughout the year.

Once school bells caused your heart to quake
As teachers circled each mistake.
Use SparkNotes and no longer weep,
Ace every single test you take.

Yes, books are lovely, dark, and deep,
But only what you grasp you keep,
With hours to go before you sleep,
With hours to go before you sleep.

CONTENTS

NOTE: This SparkNote refers to the 1998 Anchor Books edition of *The Handmaid's Tale*. The novel is arranged both by chapters (denoted by Arabic numerals) and by books (denoted by roman numerals). This SparkNote is arranged by chapter.

CONTEXT

MARGARET ATWOOD WAS BORN in Ottawa, Ontario, on November 18, 1939. She published her first book of poetry in 1961 while attending the University of Toronto. She later received degrees from both Radcliffe College and Harvard University, and pursued a career in teaching at the university level. Her first novel, *The Edible Woman,* was published in 1969 to wide acclaim. Atwood continued teaching as her literary career blossomed. She has lectured widely and has served as a writer-in-residence at colleges ranging from the University of Toronto to Macquarie University in Australia.

Atwood wrote *The Handmaid's Tale* in West Berlin and Alabama in the mid-1980s. The novel, published in 1986, quickly became a best-seller. *The Handmaid's Tale* falls squarely within the twentieth-century tradition of anti-utopian, or "dystopian" novels, exemplified by classics like Aldous Huxley's *Brave New World* and George Orwell's *1984.* Novels in this genre present imagined worlds and societies that are not ideals, but instead are terrifying or restrictive. Atwood's novel offers a strongly feminist vision of dystopia. She wrote it shortly after the elections of Ronald Reagan in the United States and Margaret Thatcher in Great Britain, during a period of conservative revival in the West partly fueled by a strong, well-organized movement of religious conservatives who criticized what they perceived as the excesses of the "sexual revolution" of the 1960s and 1970s. The growing power of this "religious right" heightened feminist fears that the gains women had made in previous decades would be reversed.

In *The Handmaid's Tale,* Atwood explores the consequences of a reversal of women's rights. In the novel's nightmare world of Gilead, a group of conservative religious extremists has taken power and turned the sexual revolution on its head. Feminists argued for liberation from traditional gender roles, but Gilead is a society founded on a "return to traditional values" and gender roles, and on the subjugation of women by men. What feminists considered the great triumphs of the 1970s—namely, widespread access to contraception, the legalization of abortion, and the increasing political influence of female voters—have all been undone. Women in Gilead are not only forbidden to vote, they are forbidden to read or write. Atwood's novel also paints a picture of a world undone by pollution and infertility, reflecting 1980s fears about declining birthrates, the dangers of nuclear power, and environmental degradation.

Some of the novel's concerns seem dated today, and its implicit condemnation of the political goals of America's religious conservatives has been criticized as unfair and overly paranoid. Nonetheless, *The Handmaid's Tale* remains one of the most powerful recent portrayals of a totalitarian society, and one of the few dystopian novels to examine in detail the intersection of politics and sexuality. The novel's exploration of the controversial politics of reproduction seems likely to guarantee Atwood's novel a readership well into the twenty-first century.

Atwood lives in Toronto with novelist Graeme Gibson and their daughter, Jess. Her most recent novel, *The Blind Assassin,* won Great Britain's Booker Prize for literature in 2000.

PLOT OVERVIEW

O FFRED IS A HANDMAID in the Republic of Gilead, a totalitarian and theocratic state that has replaced the United States of America. Because of dangerously low reproduction rates, Handmaids are assigned to bear children for elite couples that have trouble conceiving. Offred serves the Commander and his wife, Serena Joy, a former gospel singer and advocate for "traditional values." Offred is not the narrator's real name—Handmaid names consist of the word "of" followed by the name of the Handmaid's Commander. Every month, when Offred is at the right point in her menstrual cycle, she must have impersonal, wordless sex with the Commander while Serena sits behind her, holding her hands. Offred's freedom, like the freedom of all women, is completely restricted. She can leave the house only on shopping trips, the door to her room cannot be completely shut, and the Eyes, Gilead's secret police force, watch her every public move.

As Offred tells the story of her daily life, she frequently slips into flashbacks, from which the reader can reconstruct the events leading up to the beginning of the novel. In the old world, before Gilead, Offred had an affair with Luke, a married man. He divorced his wife and married Offred, and they had a child together. Offred's mother was a single mother and feminist activist. Offred's best friend, Moira, was fiercely independent. The architects of Gilead began their rise to power in an age of readily available pornography, prostitution, and violence against women—when pollution and chemical spills led to declining fertility rates. Using the military, they assassinated the president and members of Congress and launched a coup, claiming that they were taking power temporarily. They cracked down on women's rights, forbidding women to hold property or jobs. Offred and Luke took their daughter and attempted to flee across the border into Canada, but they were caught and separated from one another, and Offred has seen neither her husband nor her daughter since.

After her capture, Offred's marriage was voided (because Luke had been divorced), and she was sent to the Rachel and Leah Re-education Center, called the Red Center by its inhabitants. At the center, women were indoctrinated into Gilead's ideology in preparation for becoming Handmaids. Aunt Lydia supervised the women, giving speeches extolling Gilead's beliefs that women should be subservient to men and solely concerned with bearing children. Aunt Lydia also argued that such a social order ultimately offers women more respect and safety than the old, pre-Gilead society offered them. Moira is brought to the Red Center, but she escapes, and Offred does not know what becomes of her.

Once assigned to the Commander's house, Offred's life settles into a restrictive routine. She takes shopping trips with Ofglen, another Handmaid, and they visit the Wall outside what used to be Harvard University, where the bodies of rebels hang. She must visit the doctor frequently to be checked for disease and other complications, and she must endure the "Ceremony," in which the Commander reads to the household from the Bible, then goes to the bedroom, where his Wife and Offred wait for him, and has sex with Offred. The first break from her routine occurs when she visits the doctor and he offers to have sex with her to get her pregnant, suggesting that her Commander is probably infertile. She refuses. The doctor makes her uneasy, but his proposition is too risky—she could be sent away if caught. After a Ceremony, the Commander sends his gardener and chauffeur, Nick, to ask Offred to come see him in his study the following night. She begins visiting him regularly. They play Scrabble (which is forbidden, since women are not allowed to read), and he lets her look at old magazines like *Vogue*. At the end of these secret meetings, he asks her to kiss him.

During one of their shopping trips, Ofglen reveals to Offred that she is a member of "Mayday," an underground organization dedicated to overthrowing Gilead. Meanwhile, Offred begins to find that the Ceremony feels different and less impersonal now that she knows the Commander. Their nighttime conversations begin to touch on the new order that the Commander and his fellow leaders have created in Gilead. When Offred admits how unhappy she is, the Commander remarks, "[Y]ou can't make an omelette without breaking eggs."

After some time has gone by without Offred becoming pregnant, Serena suggests that Offred have sex with Nick secretly and pass the child off as the Commander's. Serena promises to bring Offred a picture of her daughter if she sleeps with Nick, and Offred realizes that Serena has always known the whereabouts of Offred's daughter. The same night that Offred is to sleep with Nick, the Commander secretly takes her out to a club called Jezebel's, where the

Commanders mingle with prostitutes. Offred sees Moira working there. The two women meet in a bathroom, and Offred learns that Moira was captured just before she crossed the border. She chose life in Jezebel's over being sent to the Colonies, where most political prisoners and dangerous people are sent. After that night at Jezebel's, Offred says, she never sees Moira again. The Commander takes Offred upstairs after a few hours, and they have sex in what used to be a hotel room. She tries to feign passion.

Soon after Offred returns from Jezebel's, late at night, Serena arrives and tells Offred to go to Nick's room. Offred and Nick have sex. Soon they begin to sleep together frequently, without anyone's knowledge. Offred becomes caught up in the affair and ignores Ofglen's requests that she gather information from the Commander for Mayday. One day, all the Handmaids take part in a group execution of a supposed rapist, supervised by Aunt Lydia. Ofglen strikes the first blow. Later, she tells Offred that the so-called rapist was a member of Mayday and that she hit him to put him out of his misery.

Shortly thereafter, Offred goes out shopping, and a new Ofglen meets her. This new woman is not part of Mayday, and she tells Offred that the old Ofglen hanged herself when she saw the secret police coming for her. At home, Serena has found out about Offred's trip to Jezebel's, and she sends her to her room, promising punishment. Offred waits there, and she sees a black van from the Eyes approach. Then Nick comes in and tells her that the Eyes are really Mayday members who have come to save her. Offred leaves with them, over the Commander's futile objections, on her way either to prison or to freedom—she does not know which.

The novel closes with an epilogue from 2195, after Gilead has fallen, written in the form of a lecture given by Professor Pieixoto. He explains the formation and customs of Gilead in objective, analytical language. He discusses the significance of Offred's story, which has turned up on cassette tapes in Bangor, Maine. He suggests that Nick arranged Offred's escape but that her fate after that is unknown. She could have escaped to Canada or England, or she could have been recaptured.

CHARACTER LIST

Offred   The narrator and protagonist of *The Handmaid's Tale*. Offred belongs to the class of Handmaids, fertile women forced to bear children for elite, barren couples. Handmaids show which Commander owns them by adopting their Commanders' names, such as Fred, and preceding them with "Of." Offred remembers her real name but never reveals it. She no longer has family or friends, though she has flashbacks to a time in which she had a daughter and a husband named Luke. The cruel physical and psychological burdens of her daily life in Gilead torment her and pervade her narrative.

The Commander The Commander is the head of the household where Offred works as a Handmaid. He initiates an unorthodox relationship with Offred, secretly playing Scrabble with her in his study at night. He often seems a decent, well-meaning man, and Offred sometimes finds that she likes him in spite of herself. He almost seems a victim of Gilead, making the best of a society he opposes. However, we learn from various clues and from the epilogue that the Commander was actually involved in designing and establishing Gilead.

Serena Joy The Commander's Wife, Serena worked in pre-Gilead days as a gospel singer, then as an anti-feminist activist and crusader for "traditional values." In Gilead, she sits at the top of the female social ladder, yet she is desperately unhappy. Serena's unhappiness shows that her restrictive, male-dominated society cannot bring happiness even to its most pampered and powerful women. Serena jealously guards her claims to status and behaves cruelly toward the Handmaids in her household.

Moira   Offred's best friend from college, Moira is a lesbian and a staunch feminist; she embodies female resourcefulness and independence. Her defiant nature contrasts starkly with the behavior of the other women in the novel. Rather than passively accept her fate as a Handmaid, she makes several escape attempts and finally manages to get away from the Red Center. However, she is caught before she can get out of Gilead. Later, Offred encounters Moira working as a prostitute in a club for the Commanders. At the club, Moira seems resigned to her fate, which suggests that a totalitarian society can grind down and crush even the most resourceful and independent people.

Aunt Lydia The Aunts are the class of women assigned to indoctrinate the Handmaids with the beliefs of the new society and make them accept their fates. Aunt Lydia works at the "Red Center," the re-education center where Offred and other women go for instruction before becoming Handmaids. Although she appears only in Offred's flashbacks, Aunt Lydia and her instructions haunt Offred in her daily life. Aunt Lydia's slogans and maxims drum the ideology of the new society into heads of the women, until even those like Offred, women who do not truly believe in the ideology, hear Gilead's words echoing in their heads.

Nick   Nick is a Guardian, a low-level officer of Gilead assigned to the Commander's home, where he works as a gardener and chauffeur. He and Offred have a sexual chemistry that they get to satisfy when Serena Joy orchestrates an encounter between them in an effort to get Offred pregnant. After sleeping together once, they begin a covert sexual affair. Nick is not just a Guardian; he may work either as a member of the Eyes, Gilead's secret police, or as a member of the underground Mayday resistance, or both. At the end of the novel, Nick orchestrates Offred's escape from the Commander's home, but we do not know whether he puts her into the hands of the Eyes or the resistance.

Ofglen   Another Handmaid who is Offred's shopping partner and a member of the subversive "Mayday" underground. At the end of the novel, Ofglen is found out, and she hangs herself rather than face torture and reveal the names of her co-conspirators.

Cora   Cora works as a servant in the Commander's household. She belongs to the class of Marthas, infertile women who do not qualify for the high status of Wives and so work in domestic roles. Cora seems more content with her role than her fellow Martha, Rita. She hopes that Offred will be able to conceive, because then she will have a hand in raising a child.

Janine   Offred knows Janine from their time at the Red Center. After Janine becomes a Handmaid, she takes the name Ofwarren. She has a baby, which makes her the envy of all the other Handmaids in the area, but the baby later turns out to be deformed—an "Unbaby"—and there are rumors that her doctor fathered the child. Janine is a conformist, always ready to go along with what Gilead demands of her, and so she endears herself to the Aunts and to all authority figures. Offred holds Janine in contempt for taking the easy way out.

Luke   In the days before Gilead, Luke had an affair with Offred while he was married to another woman, then got a divorce and became Offred's husband. When Gilead comes to power, he attempts to escape to Canada with Offred and their daughter, but they are captured. He is separated from Offred, and the couple never see one another again. The kind of love they shared is prohibited in Gilead, and Offred's memories of Luke contrast with the regimented, passionless state of male-female relations in the new society.

Offred's mother Offred remembers her mother in flashbacks to her pre-Gilead world—she was a single parent and a feminist activist. One day during her education at the Red Center, Offred sees a video of her mother as a young woman, yelling and carrying a banner in an anti-rape march called Take Back the Night. She embodies everything the architects of Gilead want to stamp out.

Aunt Elizabeth Aunt Elizabeth is one of the Aunts at the Red Center. Moira attacks her and steals her Aunt's uniform during her escape from the Red Center.

Rita A Martha, or domestic servant, in the Commander's household. She seems less content with her lot than Cora, the other Martha working there.

Professor Pieixoto The guest speaker at the symposium that takes place in the epilogue to *The Handmaid's Tale*. He and another academic, working at a university in the year 2195, transcribed Offred's recorded narrative; his lecture details the historical significance of the story that we have just read.

ANALYSIS OF MAJOR CHARACTERS

OFFRED

Offred is the narrator and the protagonist of the novel, and we are told the entire story from her point of view, experiencing events and memories as vividly as she does. She tells the story as it happens, and shows us the travels of her mind through asides, flashbacks, and digressions. Offred is intelligent, perceptive, and kind. She possesses enough faults to make her human, but not so many that she becomes an unsympathetic figure. She also possesses a dark sense of humor—a graveyard wit that makes her descriptions of the bleak horrors of Gilead bearable, even enjoyable. Like most of the women in Gilead, she is an ordinary woman placed in an extraordinary situation.

Offred is not a hero. Although she resists Gilead inwardly, once her attempt at escape fails, she submits outwardly. She is hardly a feminist champion; she had always felt uncomfortable with her mother's activism, and her pre-Gilead relationship with Luke began when she became his mistress, meeting him in cheap hotels for sex. Although friends with Ofglen, a member of the resistance, she is never bold enough to join up herself. Indeed, after she begins her affair with Nick, she seems to lose sight of escape entirely and suddenly feels that life in Gilead is almost bearable. If she does finally escape, it is because of Nick, not because of anything she does herself. Offred is a mostly passive character, good-hearted but complacent. Like her peers, she took for granted the freedoms feminism won and now pays the price.

THE COMMANDER

The Commander poses an ethical problem for Offred, and consequently for us. First, he is Offred's Commander and the immediate agent of her oppression. As a founder of Gilead, he also bears responsibility for the entire totalitarian society. In person, he is far more sympathetic and friendly toward Offred than most other people, and Offred's evenings with the Commander in his study offer her a small respite from the wasteland of her life. At times, his unhappiness and need for companionship make him seem as much a prisoner of Gilead's strictures as anyone else. Offred finds herself feeling sympathy for this man.

Ultimately, Offred and the reader recognize that if the Commander is a prisoner, the prison is one that he himself helped construct and that his prison is heaven compared to the prison he created for women. As the novel progresses, we come to realize that his visits with Offred are selfish rather than charitable. They satisfy his need for companionship, but he doesn't seem to care that they put Offred at terrible risk, a fact of which he must be aware, given that the previous Handmaid hanged herself when her visits to the Commander were discovered. The Commander's moral blindness, apparent in his attempts to explain the virtues of Gilead, are highlighted by his and Offred's visit to Jezebel's. The club, a place where the elite men of the society can engage in recreational extramarital sex, reveals the rank hypocrisy that runs through Gileadean society.

Offred's relationship with the Commander is best represented by a situation she remembers from a documentary on the Holocaust. In the film, the mistress of a brutal death camp guard defended the man she loved, claiming that he was not a monster. "How easy it is to invent a humanity," Offred thinks. In other words, anyone can seem human, and even likable, given the right set of circumstances. But even if the Commander is likable and can be kind or considerate, his responsibility for the creation of Gilead and his callousness to the hell he created for women means that he, like the Nazi guard, is a monster.

SERENA JOY

Though Serena had been an advocate for traditional values and the establishment of the Gileadean state, her bitterness at the outcome—being confined to the home and having to see her husband copulating with a Handmaid—suggests that spokeswomen for antifeminist causes might not enjoy getting their way as much as they believe they would. Serena's obvious unhappiness means that she teeters on the edge of inspiring our sympathy, but she forfeits that sympathy by taking out her frustration on Offred. She seems to possess no compassion for Offred. She can see the difficulty of her own life, but not that of another woman.

The climactic moment in Serena's interaction with Offred comes when she arranges for Offred to sleep with Nick. It seems that Serena makes these plans out of a desire to help Offred get pregnant, but Serena gets an equal reward from Offred's pregnancy: she gets to raise the baby. Furthermore, Serena's offer to show Offred a picture of her lost daughter if she sleeps with Nick reveals that Serena has always known of Offred's daughter's whereabouts. Not only has she cruelly concealed this knowledge, she is willing to exploit Offred's loss of a child in order to get an infant of her own. Serena's lack of sympathy makes her the perfect tool for Gilead's social order, which relies on the willingness of women to oppress other women. She is a cruel, selfish woman, and Atwood implies that such women are the glue that binds Gilead.

MOIRA

Throughout the novel, Moira's relationship with Offred epitomizes female friendship. Gilead claims to promote solidarity between women, but in fact it only produces suspicion, hostility, and petty tyranny. The kind of relationship that Moira and Offred maintain from college onward does not exist in Gilead.

In Offred's flashbacks, Moira also embodies female resistance to Gilead. She is a lesbian, which means that she rejects male-female sexual interactions, the only kind that Gilead values. More than that, she is the only character who stands up to authority directly by make two escape attempts, one successful, from the Red Center. The manner in which she escapes—taking off her clothes and putting on the uniform of an Aunt—symbolizes her rejection of Gilead's attempt to define her identity. From then on, until Offred meets up with her again, Moira represents an alternative to the meek subservience and acceptance of one's fate that most of the Handmaids adopt. When Offred runs into Moira, Moira has been recaptured and is working as a prostitute at Jezebel's, servicing the Commanders. Her fighting spirit seems broken, and she has become resigned to her fate. After embodying resistance for most of the novel, Moira comes to exemplify the way a totalitarian state can crush even the most independent spirit.

Themes, Motifs & Symbols

Themes

Themes are the fundamental and often universal ideas explored in a literary work.

Women's Bodies as Political Instruments

Because Gilead was formed in response to the crisis caused by dramatically decreased birthrates, the state's entire structure, with its religious trappings and rigid political hierarchy, is built around a single goal: control of reproduction. The state tackles the problem head-on by assuming complete control of women's bodies through their political subjugation. Women cannot vote, hold property or jobs, read, or do anything else that might allow them to become subversive or independent and thereby undermine their husbands or the state.

Despite all of Gilead's pro-women rhetoric, such subjugation creates a society in which women are treated as subhuman. They are reduced to their fertility, treated as nothing more than a set of ovaries and a womb. In one of the novel's key scenes, Offred lies in the bath and reflects that, before Gilead, she considered her body an instrument of her desires; now, she is just a mound of flesh surrounding a womb that must be filled in order to make her useful. Gilead seeks to deprive women of their individuality in order to make them docile carriers of the next generation.

Language as a Tool of Power

Gilead creates an official vocabulary that ignores and warps reality in order to serve the needs of the new society's elite. Having made it illegal for women to hold jobs, Gilead creates a system of titles. Whereas men are defined by their military rank, women are defined solely by their gender roles as Wives, Handmaids, or Marthas. Stripping them of permanent individual names strips them of their individuality, or tries to. Feminists and deformed babies are treated as subhuman, denoted by the terms "Unwomen" and "Unbabies."

Blacks and Jews are defined by biblical terms ("Children of Ham" and "Sons of Jacob," respectively) that set them apart from the rest of society, making their persecution easier. There are prescribed greetings for personal encounters, and to fail to offer the correct greetings is to fall under suspicion of disloyalty. Specially created terms define the rituals of Gilead, such as "Prayvaganzas," "Salvagings," and "Particicutions." Dystopian novels about the dangers of totalitarian society frequently explore the connection between a state's repression of its subjects and its perversion of language ("Newspeak" in George Orwell's *1984* is the most famous example), and *The Handmaid's Tale* carries on this tradition. Gilead maintains its control over women's bodies by maintaining control over names.

THE CAUSES OF COMPLACENCY

In a totalitarian state, Atwood suggests, people will endure oppression willingly as long as they receive some slight amount of power or freedom. Offred remembers her mother saying that it is "truly amazing, what people can get used to, as long as there are a few compensations." Offred's complacency after she begins her relationship with Nick shows the truth of this insight. Her situation restricts her horribly compared to the freedom her former life allowed, but her relationship with Nick allows her to reclaim the tiniest fragment of her former existence. The physical affection and companionship become compensation that make the restrictions almost bearable. Offred seems suddenly so content that she does not say yes when Ofglen asks her to gather information about the Commander.

Women in general support Gilead's existence by willingly participating in it, serving as agents of the totalitarian state. While a woman like Serena Joy has no power in the world of men, she exercises authority within her own household and seems to delight in her tyranny over Offred. She jealously guards what little power she has and wields it eagerly. In a similar way, the women known as Aunts, especially Aunt Lydia, act as willing agents of the Gileadean state. They indoctrinate other women into the ruling ideology, keep a close eye out for rebellion, and generally serve the same function for Gilead that the Jewish police did under Nazi rule.

Atwood's message is bleak. At the same time as she condemns Offred, Serena Joy, the Aunts, and even Moira for their complacency, she suggests that even if those women mustered strength and stopped complying, they would likely fail to make a difference. In

Gilead the tiny rebellions of resistances do not necessarily matter. In the end, Offred escapes because of luck rather than resistance.

MOTIFS

Motifs are recurring structures, contrasts, or literary devices that can help to develop and inform the text's major themes.

RAPE AND SEXUAL VIOLENCE

Sexual violence, particularly against women, pervades *The Handmaid's Tale*. The prevalence of rape and pornography in the pre-Gilead world justified to the founders their establishment of the new order. The Commander and the Aunts claim that women are better protected in Gilead, that they are treated with respect and kept safe from violence. Certainly, the official penalty for rape is terrible: in one scene, the Handmaids tear apart with their bare hands a supposed rapist (actually a member of the resistance). Yet, while Gilead claims to suppress sexual violence, it actually institutionalizes it, as we see at Jezebel's, the club that provides the Commanders with a ready stable of prostitutes to service the male elite. Most important, sexual violence is apparent in the central institution of the novel, the Ceremony, which compels Handmaids to have sex with their Commanders.

RELIGIOUS TERMS USED FOR POLITICAL PURPOSES

Gilead is a theocracy—a government in which there is no separation between state and religion—and its official vocabulary incorporates religious terminology and biblical references. Domestic servants are called "Marthas" in reference to a domestic character in the New Testament; the local police are "Guardians of the Faith"; soldiers are "Angels"; and the Commanders are officially "Commanders of the Faithful." All the stores have biblical names: Loaves and Fishes, All Flesh, Milk and Honey. Even the automobiles have biblical names like Behemoth, Whirlwind, and Chariot. Using religious terminology to describe people, ranks, and businesses whitewashes political skullduggery in pious language. It provides an ever-present reminder that the founders of Gilead insist they act on the authority of the Bible itself. Politics and religion sleep in the same bed in Gilead, where the slogan "God is a National Resource" predominates.

SIMILARITIES BETWEEN
REACTIONARY AND FEMINIST IDEOLOGIES

Although *The Handmaid's Tale* offers a specifically feminist critique of the reactionary attitudes toward women that hold sway in Gilead, Atwood occasionally draws similarities between the architects of Gilead and radical feminists such as Offred's mother. Both groups claim to protect women from sexual violence, and both show themselves willing to restrict free speech in order to accomplish this goal. Offred recalls a scene in which her mother and other feminists burn porn magazines. Like the founders of Gilead, these feminists ban some expressions of sexuality. Gilead also uses the feminist rhetoric of female solidarity and "sisterhood" to its own advantage. These points of similarity imply the existence of a dark side of feminist rhetoric. Despite Atwood's gentle criticism of the feminist left, her real target is the religious right.

SYMBOLS

> *Symbols are objects, characters, figures, or colors used to represent abstract ideas or concepts.*

CAMBRIDGE, MASSACHUSETTS

The center of Gilead's power, where Offred lives, is never explicitly identified, but a number of clues mark it as the town of Cambridge. Cambridge, its neighboring city of Boston, and Massachusetts as a whole were centers for America's first religious and intolerant society—the Puritan New England of the seventeenth century. Atwood reminds us of this history with the ancient Puritan church that Offred and Ofglen visit early in the novel, which Gilead has turned into a museum. The choice of Cambridge as a setting symbolizes the direct link between the Puritans and their spiritual heirs in Gilead. Both groups dealt harshly with religious, sexual, or political deviation.

HARVARD UNIVERSITY

Gilead has transformed Harvard's buildings into a detention center run by the Eyes, Gilead's secret police. Bodies of executed dissidents hang from the Wall that runs around the college, and Salvagings (mass executions) take place in Harvard Yard, on the steps of the library. Harvard becomes a symbol of the inverted world that Gilead has created: a place that was founded to pursue knowledge and truth becomes a seat of oppression, torture, and the denial of every principle for which a university is supposed to stand.

THE HANDMAIDS' RED HABITS

The red color of the costumes worn by the Handmaids symbolizes fertility, which is the caste's primary function. Red suggests the blood of the menstrual cycle and of childbirth. At the same time, however, red is also a traditional marker of sexual sin, hearkening back to the scarlet letter worn by the adulterous Hester Prynne in Nathaniel Hawthorne's tale of Puritan ideology. While the Handmaids' reproductive role supposedly finds its justification in the Bible, in some sense they commit adultery by having sex with their Commanders, who are married men. The wives, who often call the Handmaids sluts, feel the pain of this sanctioned adultery. The Handmaids' red garments, then, also symbolize the ambiguous sinfulness of the Handmaids' position in Gilead.

A PALIMPSEST

A palimpsest is a document on which old writing has been scratched out, often leaving traces, and new writing put in its place; it can also be a document consisting of many layers of writing simply piled one on top of another. Offred describes the Red Center as a palimpsest, but the word actually symbolizes all of Gilead. The old world has been erased and replaced, but only partially, by a new order. Remnants of the pre-Gilead days continue to infuse the new world.

THE EYES

The Eyes of God are Gilead's secret police. Both their name and their insignia, a winged eye, symbolize the eternal watchfulness of God and the totalitarian state. In Gilead's theocracy, the eye of God and of the state are assumed to be one and the same.

SYMBOLS

SUMMARY & ANALYSIS

CHAPTERS 1–5

SUMMARY: CHAPTER 1

The narrator, whose name we learn later is Offred, describes how she and other women slept on army cots in a gymnasium. Aunt Sara and Aunt Elizabeth patrol with electric cattle prods hanging from their leather belts, and the women, forbidden to speak aloud, whisper without attracting attention. Twice daily, the women walk in the former football field, which is surrounded by a chain-link fence topped with barbed wire. Armed guards called Angels patrol outside. While the women take their walks, the Angels stand outside the fence with their backs to the women. The women long for the Angels to turn and see them. They imagine that if the men looked at them or talked to them, they could use their bodies to make a deal. The narrator describes lying in bed at night, quietly exchanging names with the other women.

SUMMARY: CHAPTER 2

The scene changes, and the story shifts from the past to the present tense. Offred now lives in a room fitted out with curtains, a pillow, a framed picture, and a braided rug. There is no glass in the room, not even over the framed picture. The window does not open completely, and the windowpane is shatterproof. There is nothing in the room from which one could hang a rope, and the door does not lock or even shut completely. Looking around, Offred remembers how Aunt Lydia told her to consider her circumstances a privilege, not a prison.

Handmaids, to which group the narrator belongs, dress entirely in red, except for the white wings framing their faces. Household servants, called "Marthas," wear green uniforms. "Wives" wear blue uniforms. Offred often secretly listens to Rita and Cora, the Marthas who work in the house where she lives. Once, she hears Rita state that she would never debase herself as someone in Offred's position must. Cora replies that Offred works for all the women, and that if she (Cora) were younger and had not gotten her tubes tied, she could have been in Offred's situation. Offred wishes she could talk to them, but Marthas are not supposed to develop relationships with Handmaids. She wishes that she could share gossip like they do—gossip about how one Handmaid gave birth to a stillborn, how a Wife stabbed a Handmaid with a knitting needle out of jealousy, how someone poisoned her Commander with toilet cleaner. Offred dresses for a shopping trip. She collects from Rita the tokens that serve as currency. Each token bears an image of what it will purchase: twelve eggs, cheese, and a steak.

SUMMARY: CHAPTER 3

On her way out, Offred looks around for the Commander's Wife but does not see her. The Commander's Wife has a garden, and she knits constantly. All the Wives knit scarves "for the Angels at the front lines," but the Commander's Wife is a particularly skilled knitter. Offred wonders if the scarves actually get used, or if they just give the Wives something to do. She remembers arriving at the Commander's house for the first time, after the two couples to which she was previously assigned "didn't work out." One of the Wives in an earlier posting secluded herself in the bedroom, purportedly drinking, and Offred hoped the new Commander's Wife would be different. On the first day, her new mistress told her to stay out of her sight as much as possible, and to avoid making trouble. As she talked, the Wife smoked a cigarette, a black-market item. Handmaids, Offred notes, are forbidden coffee, cigarettes, and alcohol. Then the Wife reminded Offred that the Commander is *her* husband, permanently and forever. "It's one of the things we fought for," she said, looking away. Suddenly, Offred recognized her mistress as Serena Joy, the lead soprano from Growing Souls Gospel Hour, a Sunday-morning religious program that aired when Offred was a child.

ANALYSIS: CHAPTERS 1–5

The Handmaid's Tale plunges immediately into an unfamiliar, unexplained world, using unfamiliar terms like "Handmaid," "Angel," and "Commander" that only come to make sense as the story progresses. Offred gradually delivers information about her past and the world in which she lives, often narrating through flashbacks. She narrates these flashbacks in the past tense, which distinguishes them from the main body of the story, which she tells in the present tense. The first scene, in the gymnasium, is a flashback, as are Offred's memories of the Marthas' gossip and her first meeting with the Commander's Wife. Although at this point we do not know what the gymnasium signifies, or why the narrator and other women lived there, we do gather some information from the brief first chapter. The women in the gymnasium live under the constant surveillance of the Angels and the Aunts, and they cannot interact with one another. They seem to inhabit a kind of prison. Offred likens the gym to a palimpsest, a parchment either erased and written on again or layered with multiple writings. In the gym palimpsest, Offred sees multiple layers of history: high school girls going to basketball games and dances wearing miniskirts, then pants, then green hair. Likening the gym to a palimpsest also suggests that the society Offred now inhabits has been superimposed on a previous society, and traces of the old linger beneath the new.

In Chapter 2, Offred sits in a room that seems at first like a pleasant change from harsh atmosphere of the gymnasium. However, her description of her room demonstrates that the same rigid, controlling structures that ruled the gym continue to constrict her in this house. The room is like a prison in which all means of defense, or escape by suicide or flight, have been removed. She wonders if women everywhere get issued exactly the same sheets and curtains, which underlines the idea that the room is like a government-ordered prison.

We do not know yet what purpose Offred serves in the house, although it seems to be sexual—Cora comments that she could have done Offred's work if she hadn't gotten her tubes tied, which implies that Offred's function is reproductive. Serena Joy's coldness to Offred makes it plain that she considers Offred a threat, or at least an annoyance. We do know from Offred's name that she, like all Handmaids, is considered state property. Handmaids' names simply reflect which Commander owns them. "Of Fred," "Of Warren," and "Of Glen" get collapsed into "Offred," "Ofwarren," and "Ofglen." The names make more sense when preceded by the word "Property": "Property Offred," for example. Thus, every time the women hear their names, they are reminded that they are no more than property.

These early chapters establish the novel's style, which is characterized by considerable physical description. The narrator devotes attention to the features of the gym, the Commander's house, and Serena Joy's pinched face. Offred tells the story in nonlinear fashion, following the temporal leaps of her own mind. The narrative

SUMMARY & ANALYSIS

goes where her thoughts take it—one moment to the present, in the Commander's house, and the next back in the gymnasium, or in the old world, the United States as it exists in Offred's memory. We do not have the sense, as in some first-person narratives, that Offred is composing this story from a distanced vantage point, reflecting back on her past. Rather, all of her thoughts have a quality of immediacy. We are there with Offred as she goes about her daily life, and as she slips out of the present and thinks about her past.

CHAPTERS 4–6

SUMMARY: CHAPTER 4

As she leaves the house to go shopping, Offred notices Nick, a Guardian of the Faith, washing the Commander's car. Nick lives above the garage. He winks at Offred—an offense against decorum— but she ignores him, fearing that he may be an Eye, a spy assigned to test her. She waits at the corner for Ofglen, another Handmaid with whom Offred will do her shopping. The Handmaids always travel in pairs when outside.

Ofglen arrives, and they exchange greetings, careful not to say anything that isn't strictly orthodox. Ofglen says that she has heard the war is going well, and that the army recently defeated a group of Baptist rebels. "Praise be," Offred responds. They reach a checkpoint manned by two young Guardians. The Guardians serve as a routine police force and do menial labor. They are men too young, too old, or just generally unfit for the army. Young Guardians, such as these, can be dangerous because they are frequently more fanatical or nervous than older guards. These young Guardians recently shot a Martha as she fumbled for her pass, because they thought she was a man in disguise carrying a bomb. Offred heard Rita and Cora talking about the shooting. Rita was angry, but Cora seemed to accept the shooting as the price one pays for safety.

At the checkpoint, Offred subtly flirts with one of the Guardians by making eye contact, cherishing this small infraction against the rules. She considers how sex-starved the young men must be, since they cannot marry without permission, masturbation is a sin, and pornographic magazines and films are now forbidden. The Guardians can only hope to become Angels, when they will be allowed to take a wife and perhaps eventually get a Handmaid. This marks the first time in the novel we hear the word "Handmaid" used.

SUMMARY: CHAPTER 5

In town, Ofglen and Offred wait in line at the shops. We learn the name of this new society: "The Republic of Gilead." Offred remembers the pre-Gilead days, when women were not protected: they had to keep their doors closed to strangers and ignore catcalls on the street. Now no one whistles at women as they walk; no one touches them or talks to them. She remembers Aunt Lydia explaining that more than one kind of freedom exists, and that "[i]n the days of anarchy, it was freedom to. Now you are being given freedom from."

The women shop at stores known by names like All Flesh and Milk and Honey. Pictures of meat or fruit mark the stores, rather than lettered signs, because "they decided that even the names of shops were too much temptation for us." A Handmaid in the late stages of pregnancy enters the store and raises a flurry of excitement. Offred recognizes her from the Red Center. She used to be known as Janine, and she was one of Aunt Lydia's favorites. Now her name is Ofwarren. Offred senses that Janine went shopping just so she could show off her pregnancy.

Offred thinks of her husband, Luke, and their daughter, and the life they led before Gilead existed. She remembers a prosaic detail from their everyday life together: she used to store plastic shopping bags under the sink, which annoyed Luke, who worried that their daughter would get one of the bags caught over her head. She remembers feeling guilty for her carelessness. Offred and Ofglen finish their shopping and go out to the sidewalk, where they encounter a group of Japanese tourists and their interpreter. The tourists want to take a photograph, but Offred says no. Many of the interpreters are Eyes, and Handmaids must not appear immodest. Offred and Ofglen marvel at the women's exposed legs, high heels, and polished toenails. The tourists ask if they are happy, and since Ofglen does not answer, Offred replies that they are very happy.

SUMMARY: CHAPTER 6

> *This may not seem ordinary to you now, but after a time it will. It will become ordinary.*
>
> (See QUOTATIONS, p. 67)

As they return from shopping, Ofglen suggests they take the long way and pass by the church. It is an old building, decorated inside with paintings of what seem to be Puritans from the colonial era. Now the former church is kept as a museum. Offred describes a nearby boathouse, old dormitories, a football stadium, and red-brick sidewalks. Atwood implies that Offred is walking across what used to be the campus of Harvard University. Across the street from the church sits the Wall, where the authorities hang the bodies of executed criminals as examples to the rest of the Republic of Gilead. The authorities cover the men's heads with bags. One of the bags looks painted with a red smile where the blood has seeped through. All of the six corpses wear signs around their necks picturing fetuses, signaling that they were executed for performing abortions before Gilead came into existence. Although their actions were legal at the time, their crimes are being punished retroactively. Offred feels relieved that none of the bodies could be Luke's, since he was not a doctor. As she stares at the bodies, Offred thinks of Aunt Lydia telling them that soon their new life would seem ordinary.

ANALYSIS: CHAPTERS 4–6

The theocratic nature of Offred's society, the name of which we learn for the first time in these chapters, becomes clear during her shopping trip. A theocracy exists when there is no separation between church and state, and a single religion dominates all aspects of life. In Gilead, state and religion are inseparable. The official language of Gilead uses many biblical terms, from the various ranks that men hold (Angels, Guardians of the Faith, Commanders of the Faith, the Eyes of God), to the stores where Offred and Ofglen shop (Milk and Honey, All Flesh, Loaves and Fishes), to the names of automobiles (Behemoth, Whirlwind, Chariot). The very name "Gilead" refers to a location in ancient Israel. The name also recalls a line from the Book of Psalms: "there is a balm in Gilead." This phrase, we realize later, has been transformed into a kind of national motto.

Atwood does not describe the exact details of Gilead's state religion. In Chapter 2, Offred describes her room as "a return to traditional values." The religious right in America uses the phrase "traditional values," so Atwood seems to link the values of this dystopic society to the values of the Protestant Christian religious right in America. Gilead seems more Protestant than anything else, but its brand of Christianity pays far more attention to the Old Testament than the New Testament. The religious justification for having Handmaids, for instance, is taken from the Book of Genesis. We learn that neither Catholics nor Jews are welcome in Gilead. The former must convert, while the latter must emigrate to Israel or renounce their Judaism.

Atwood seems less interested in religion than in the intersection between religion, politics, and sex. *The Handmaid's Tale* explores the political oppression of women, carried out in the name of God but in large part motivated by a desire to control women's bodies. Gilead sees women's sexuality as dangerous: women must cover themselves from head to toe, for example, and not reveal their sexual attractions. When Offred attracts the Guardians, she feels this ability to inspire sexual attraction is the only power she retains. Every other privilege is stripped away, down to the very act of reading, which is forbidden. Women are not even allowed to read store signs. By controlling women's minds, by not allowing them to read, the authorities more easily control women's bodies. The patriarchs of Gilead want to control women's bodies, their sex lives, and their reproductive rights. The bodies of slain abortionists on the Wall hammer home the point: feminists believe that women must have abortion rights in order to control their own bodies, and in Gilead, giving women control of their bodies is a horrifying crime.

When Offred and Ofglen go to town to shop, geographical clues and street names suggest that they live in what was once Cambridge, Massachusetts, and that their walk takes them near what used to be the campus of Harvard University. The choice of Cambridge for the setting of *The Handmaid's Tale* is significant, since Massachusetts was a Puritan stronghold during the colonial period of the United States. The Puritans were a persecuted minority in England, but when they fled to New England, they re-created the repression they suffered at home, this time casting themselves as the repressors rather than the repressed. They established an intolerant religious society in some ways similar to Gilead. Atwood locates her fictional intolerant society in a place founded by intolerant people. By turning the old church into a museum, and leaving untouched portraits of Puritan forebears, the founders of Gilead suggest their admiration for the old Puritan society.

CHAPTERS 7–9

SUMMARY: CHAPTER 7

> *I would like to believe this is a story I'm telling. I need to believe it. I must believe it. Those who can believe that such stories are only stories have a better chance.*
>
> (See QUOTATIONS, p. 68)

At night, Offred likes to remember her former life. She recalls talking to her college friend, Moira, in her dorm room. She remembers being a child and going to a park with her mother, where they saw a group of women and a few men burning pornographic magazines. Offred has forgotten a large chunk of time, which she thinks might be the fault of an injection or pill the authorities gave her. She remembers waking up somewhere and screaming, demanding to know what they had done with her daughter. The authorities told Offred she was unfit, and her daughter was with those fit to care for her. They showed her a photograph of her child wearing a white dress, holding the hand of a strange woman. As she recounts these events, Offred imagines she is telling her story to someone, telling things that she cannot write down, because writing is forbidden.

SUMMARY: CHAPTER 8

Returning from another shopping trip, Ofglen and Offred notice three new bodies on the Wall. One is a Catholic priest and two are Guardians who bear placards around their necks that read "Gender Treachery." This means they were hanged for committing homosexual acts. After looking at the bodies for a while, Offred tells Ofglen that they should continue walking home. They meet a funeral procession of Econowives, the wives of poorer men. One Econowife carries a small black jar. From the size of the jar, Offred can tell that it contains a dead embryo from an early miscarriage— one that came too early to know whether it was an "Unbaby." The Econowives do not like the Handmaids. One woman scowls, and another spits at the Handmaids as they pass.

At the corner near the Commander's home, Ofglen says "Under His Eye," the orthodox good-bye, hesitating as if she wants to say more but then continuing on her way. When Offred reaches the Commander's driveway she passes Nick, who breaks the rules by asking her about her walk. She says nothing and goes into the house.

She sees Serena Joy out in the garden and recalls how after Serena's singing career ended, she became a spokesperson for respecting the "sanctity of the home" and for women staying at home instead of working. Serena herself never stayed at home, because she was always out giving speeches. Once, Offred remembers, someone tried to assassinate Serena but killed her secretary instead. Offred wonders if Serena is angry that she can no longer be a public figure, now that what she advocated has come to pass and all women, including her, are confined to the home.

In the kitchen, Rita fusses over the quality of the purchases as she always does. Offred retreats upstairs and notices the Commander standing outside her room. He is not supposed to be there. He nods at her and retreats.

Summary: Chapter 9

Offred remembers renting hotel rooms and waiting for Luke to meet her, before they were married, when he was cheating on his first wife. She regrets that she did not fully appreciate the freedom to have her own space when she wanted it. Thinking of the problems she and Luke thought they had, she realizes they were truly happy, although they did not know it. She remembers examining her room in the Commander's house little by little after she first arrived. She saw stains on the mattress, left over from long-ago sex, and she discovered a Latin phrase freshly scratched into the floor of the closet: *Nolite te bastardes carborundorum*. Offred does not understand Latin. It pleases her to imagine that this message allows her to commune with the woman who wrote it. She pictures this woman as freckly and irreverent, someone like Moira. Later, she asks Rita who stayed in her room before her. Rita tells her to specify which one, implying that there were a number of Handmaids before her. Offred says, guessing, "[t]he lively one . . . with freckles." Rita asks how Offred knew about her, but she refuses to tell Offred anything about the previous Handmaid beyond a vague statement that she did not work out.

Analysis: Chapter 7–9

Atwood suggests that those who seek to restrict sexual expression, whether they are feminists or religious conservatives, ultimately share the same goal—the control of sexuality, particularly women's sexuality. In the flashback to the scene from Offred's childhood in which women burn pornographic magazines, Atwood shows the similarity between the extremism of the left and the extremism of the right. The people burning magazines are feminists, not religious conservatives like the leaders of Gilead, yet their goal is the same: to crack down on certain kinds of sexual freedom. In other words, the desire for control over sexuality is not unique to the religious totalitarians of Gilead; it also existed in the feminist anti-pornography crusades that preceded the fall of the United States. Gilead actually appropriates some of the rhetoric of women's liberation in its attempt to control women. Gilead also uses the Aunts and the Aunts' rhetoric, forcing women to control other women. Again and again in the novel, the voice of Aunt Lydia rings in Offred's head, insisting that women are better off in Gilead, free from exploitation and violence, than they were in the dangerous freedom of pre-Gilead times.

In Chapter 7, Offred relates some of the details of how she lost her child. This loss is the central wound on Offred's psyche throughout the novel, and the novel's great source of emotional power. The loss of her child is so painful to Offred that she can only relate the story in fits and starts; so far the details of what happened have been murky. When telling stories from her past, like the story of her daughter's disappearance, Offred often seems to draw on a partial or foggy memory. It almost seems as if she is remembering details from hundreds of years ago, when we know these things happened a few years before the narrative. Partly this distance is the product of emotional trauma—thinking of the past is painful for Offred. But in Chapter 7, Offred offers her own explanation for these gaps: she thinks it possible that the authorities gave her a pill or injection that harmed her memory.

Immediately after remembering her daughter, Offred addresses someone she calls "you." She could be talking to God, Luke, or an imaginary future reader. "I would like to believe this is a story I'm telling," Offred says. "Those who can believe that such stories are only stories have a better chance . . . A story is a letter. *Dear You*, I'll say." In the act of telling her imagined audience about her life, Offred reduces her life's horror and makes its oppressive weight endurable. Also, if she can think of her life as a story and herself as the writer, she can think of her life as controllable, fictional, something not terrifying because not real.

We learn in Chapter 8 that Serena used to campaign against women's rights. This makes her a figure worthy of pity, in a way;

she supported the anti-woman principles on which Gilead was founded, but once they were implemented, she found that they affected her as well as other women. She now lives deprived of freedom and saddled with a Handmaid who has sex with her husband. Yet Serena forfeits what pity we might feel for her by her callous, petty behavior toward Offred. Powerless in the world of men, Serena can only take out her frustration on the women under her thumb by making their lives miserable. In many ways, she treats Offred far worse than the Commander does, which suggests that Gilead's oppressive power structure succeeds not just because men created it, but because women like Serena sustain it.

Nolite te bastardes carborundorum—the Latin phrase scrawled in Offred's closet by a previous Handmaid—takes on a magical importance for Offred even before she knows what it means. It symbolizes her inner resistance to Gilead's tyranny and makes her feel like she can communicate with other strong women, like the woman who wrote the message. In Chapter 29 we learn what the phrase means, and its role in sustaining Offred's resistance comes to seem perfectly appropriate.

CHAPTERS 10–12

SUMMARY: CHAPTER 10

Offred often sings songs in her head—"Amazing Grace" or songs by Elvis. Most music is forbidden in Gilead, and there is little of it in the Commander's home. Sometimes she hears Serena humming and listening to a recording of herself from the time when she was a famous gospel singer. Summer is approaching, and the house grows hot. Soon the Handmaids will be allowed to wear their summer dresses. Offred thinks about how Aunt Lydia would describe the terrible things that used to happen to women in the old days, before Gilead, when they sunbathed wearing next to nothing. Offred remembers Moira throwing an "underwhore" party to sell sexy lingerie. She remembers reading stories in the papers about women who were murdered and raped, but even in the old days it seemed distant from her life and unrelated to her. Offred sits at the window, beside a cushion embroidered with the word FAITH. It is the only word they have given her to read, and she spends many minutes looking at it. From her window, she watches the Commander get into his car and drive away.

SUMMARY: CHAPTER 11

Offred says that yesterday she went to the doctor. Every month, a Guardian accompanies Offred to a doctor, who tests her for pregnancy and disease. At the doctor's office, Offred undresses, pulling a sheet over her body. A sheet hangs down from the ceiling, cutting off the doctor's view of her face. The doctor is not supposed to see her face or speak to her if he can help it. On this visit, though, he chatters cheerfully and then offers to help her. He says many of the Commanders are either too old to produce a child or are sterile, and he suggests that he could have sex with her and impregnate her. His use of the word "sterile" shocks Offred, for officially sterile men no longer exist. In Gilead, there are only fruitful women and barren women. Offred thinks him genuinely sympathetic to her plight, but she also realizes he enjoys his own empathy and his position of power. After a moment, she declines, saying it is too dangerous. If they are caught, they will both receive the death penalty. She tries to sound casual and grateful as she refuses, but she feels frightened. To revenge her refusal, the doctor could falsely report that she has a health problem, and then she would be sent to the Colonies with the "Unwomen." Offred also feels frightened, she realizes, because she has been given a way out.

SUMMARY: CHAPTER 12

It is one of Offred's required bath days. The bathroom has no mirror, no razors, and no lock on the door. Cora sits outside, waiting for Offred. Offred's own naked body seems strange to her, and she finds it hard to believe that she once wore bathing suits, letting people see her thighs and arms, her breasts and buttocks. Lying in the bath, she thinks of her daughter and remembers the time when a crazy woman tried to kidnap the little girl in the supermarket. The authorities in Gilead took Offred's then-five-year-old child from her, and three years have passed since then. Offred has no mementos of her daughter. She remembers Aunt Lydia saying women should not get attached to things, and should "cultivate poverty of spirit." Aunt Lydia cited the biblical sentiment "Blessed are the meek," but she did not go on, as the Bible does, to add "for they shall inherit the earth."

Sometimes Offred thinks of her daughter as a ghost. She muses that the authorities were right: it is easier to think of your stolen children as dead. Cora, impatient, calls to her, and Offred gets out the bath. She looks down at her ankle, and sees the tattoo that Gilead places on all Handmaids. After the bath, she eats dinner, even though she does not feel hungry. The food is bland. Offred remembers Aunt Lydia saying that Handmaids are not allowed coffee, alcohol, or nicotine. She thinks of Serena and the Commander, eating below her, and wonders if the Commander ever notices his Wife. Handmaids are not allowed to keep uneaten food, but Offred wraps a pat of butter in a piece of the napkin and hides it in her shoe.

Analysis: Chapters 10–12

By this point in the novel, plentiful clues have clarified the Handmaids' role. Serena's hatred of Offred, the Handmaids' obsession with fertility ("Blessed be the fruit"; "May the Lord open" is how Handmaids greet one another), the references to declining birthrates, and the visit to the doctor all suggest that Handmaids exist to bear the children of their Commanders. In this extremely patriarchal world, men cannot be called sterile. If a woman fails to conceive, she is labeled "barren," and no one considers that the man's sterility may have been the reason. Gilead adopts premodern beliefs and rejects modern science in order to glorify men. Yet the doctor's comments to Offred show that the belief is adopted only *officially*. Privately, people realize that men, especially older men like the Commanders, can be sterile.

The doctor's offer to Offred suggests the limits of totalitarianism, and the inability of any state to control human society. Ideology may decree that Commanders can father children, but it cannot make infertile men fertile. It may outlaw the word "sterile," but people realize sterility exists. It may outlaw sexual impulses and passion, but men like the doctor still lust for strange women. Outlawed activities go on beneath Gilead's surface, including the secret impregnation of fertile women by lower-class men like the doctor. The universal need for children is central to the novel—in one way or another, it motivates all the characters. Arguably, the need for children created Gilead's entire oppressive system.

When the doctor suggests impregnating Offred, she realizes it scares her not just because the doctor could punish her if he chose to do so, but because he has offered her an escape. Offred's fear seems inexplicable at first—how could she not long to escape?—but it illustrates the prisoner mentality that sometimes overtakes her. She wants to survive, and the best way to survive is to learn to bear her chains. When she bears them too well, they become almost comforting to her. Her captivity becomes familiar, and the prospect of a new, free life becomes scary.

Aunt Lydia's words to the women suggest that Gilead operates not just by using ideas from the women's movement, but by using and perverting biblical ideas and language. She tells the women, "Blessed are the meek," but she leaves out the pivotal phrase with which the Bible ends that sentence: "for they shall inherit the earth." The Bible suggests that the downtrodden can look forward to an eternal reward—rising up against their oppressors—but the ideology of Gilead suggests just the opposite: women's glory comes from their meekness, and they will always be meek. That women would rise up against their oppressors is—beyond sinful—unthinkable. Gilead uses biblical language when convenient, even if that means taking phrases out of context and destroying their intended meaning.

In the household, a mood of loneliness and isolation exists. As a Handmaid, Offred is not only denied friends, she is denied a family. She must eat dinner apart from the rest of the household; her baths and movements are regulated as if she is an animal; the servants hardly speak to her. Without meaningful contact in the present, Offred spends much of her time remembering her past. Her memory of her daughter's attempted kidnapping in the supermarket is a piece of retrospective foreshadowing, a memory of an event that foreshadowed the ultimate loss of her daughter to some unknown woman in Gilead, who, like the supermarket madwoman, did not have a daughter and wanted one by any means necessary.

CHAPTERS 13–15

SUMMARY: CHAPTER 13

I'm a cloud, congealed around a central object, the shape of a pear, which is hard and more real than I am and glows red within its translucent wrapping.

(See QUOTATIONS, p. 69)

After dinner, Offred feels bored. She remembers paintings of harems: she used to think they were about eroticism but now realizes they depicted the boredom of the women. She wonders if men find bored women erotic. She thinks of the Red Center, and how Moira was brought there three weeks after her own arrival. Moira and Offred pretended not to know one another because friendships aroused suspicion. They arranged to meet in the restroom to exchange a few words, which made Offred feel terribly happy. At the Center everyone had to "Testify" about their past lives. Janine testified that she was gang-raped at fourteen. After she finished speaking, the Aunts asked the group whose fault the rape was, and the rest of the Handmaids chanted in unison that it was Janine's fault because she led them on. When she cried, they called her a crybaby.

Offred says she used to think of her body as an instrument of pleasure or of transportation, an instrument she controlled. Now, others define her body as nothing more than a uterus. She hates facing menstruation every month because it means failure. Her only function is childbearing. Offred remembers running through the woods, trying to escape with her daughter. She could not run very fast, because her child slowed her down. She remembers hearing shots. She and her daughter fell to the ground, hiding; Offred begged her daughter to be quiet, but she was too young to understand. She remembers being physically restrained and watching her daughter get dragged away from her.

SUMMARY: CHAPTER 14

After bathing and eating, Offred must attend the Ceremony with the rest of the household. The Commander is always late for the Ceremony. Serena sits while Offred kneels on the floor. Rita, Cora, and Nick stand behind Offred. Nick's shoe touches Offred's. She shifts her foot away, but he moves his foot so it touches hers again. As usual, Serena allows them to watch the news while they wait. Television stations from Canada are blocked, and most of the programming is religious. The news reports that spies were caught smuggling "national resources" across the border, and that five Quakers have been arrested. The newscaster declares that the "resettlement of the Children of Ham" is proceeding, with thousands of people forced to resettle in the Dakotas.

Offred remembers how she and Luke purchased fake passports when they decided to escape. They told their daughter they were going on a picnic and planned to give her a sleeping pill when they crossed the border so that she would not be questioned or give them away. They packed nothing in their car because they did not want to arouse suspicion.

SUMMARY: CHAPTER 15

The Commander arrives and proceeds to unlock an ornate box. He takes out a Bible and reads to everyone. Offred wonders what it is like to be a man like him, surrounded by women who watch his every move. The Commander reads passages that emphasize childbearing. As the Commander reads, his Wife begins to sob softly. The Commander reads the story of Rachel and Leah from the book of Genesis. Rachel was barren, so she urged her husband to have a child by her maid, Bilhah. At the Red Center, this story was drilled into the Handmaids. During lunch, they played recordings of a male voice reciting the Beatitudes, so the Aunts would not have to commit the sin of reading. Offred remembers the time when Moira decided to fake an illness, hoping to escape by bribing one of the men in the ambulance with sex. When she tried it on an Angel, he reported her. The Aunts tortured Moira by beating her feet with steel cables, the punishment for a first offense. The punishment for a second offense was beating the hands. Aunt Lydia reminded the women that hands and feet did not matter for their purpose.

ANALYSIS: CHAPTERS 13–15

If some of Gilead's rhetoric borrows from the feminist movement, some of it utterly contradicts the feminist movement. We see this when Offred remembers the group taunting of Janine. When Janine tells the story of her gang-rape at the age of fourteen, the group, at Aunt Lydia's prompting, chants that the rape was Janine's fault, that she led them on, that God allowed the rape to happen in order to teach Janine a lesson. These sentiments contrast with those espoused by feminists, who fight against blaming the victim of sexual violence and argue that leading someone on never justifies rape. This incident also illustrates the way Gilead turns women against women. Testifying is a powerful way of breaking women, for they are blamed not by their oppressors, men, but by their fellows in oppression, women. The effectiveness of the group condemnation becomes clear when Offred relates that the next week, Janine said without prompting that the rape was her fault because she led them on. These women are coerced into condemning their peer, because they know they will be punished if they do not. Horribly, however, they begin to enjoy the condemnation. When they call Janine a crybaby, Offred says, "We meant it, which was the bad part." They despise her weakness, and for a moment they truly believe the ideology Aunt Lydia feeds them.

The bath scene shows us how Offred's view of her body has changed, and more generally how women think of themselves differently in the new world. Before, Offred's body was an "instrument" for living; in Gilead its only importance is as a "cloud, congealed around her central object." That central object is her womb, which is the only part of a woman that matters in Gilead. This idea that only the womb matters gets reinforced when Offred remembers Aunt Lydia's saying hands and feet are not even necessary for Handmaids. Aunt Lydia implies that only the wombs matter, and other body parts can safely be flayed and beaten. Pain and emotion do not matter; only childbearing does.

Offred's flashbacks continue to flesh out the story of her life before becoming a Handmaid. Few people appear in Offred's flashbacks—only Luke, Moira, Offred's mother, and her daughter make appearances. Each of these characters fulfills a different human need. Moira satisfies the need for friendship, Offred's mother the need for family, her daughter the need for children, Luke the need for romantic love. Offred must satisfy her human needs as best she can by living partially in the past, for none of her needs can be satisfied in her new life.

We also learn more about the time before Gilead when Serena Joy turns on the news before the Ceremony. Previous chapters imply that Gilead is at war, and on the news we see images of the war and of subversives, and we hear reports of victories. The fact of the war is important because it suggests that Gilead does not rule everywhere—somewhere, the possibility of escape exists. The fact that subversives exist also gives hope; even if many are arrested, the fact that anyone still resists the government is encouraging. The newscaster makes reference to the "Children of Ham" and their resettlement, which touches on the subject of race. Racist ideologies of the nineteenth century often held that blacks descended from the biblical figure of Ham, who was cursed by his father, Noah, and made to be a servant of his brothers. The resettlement of this group calls to mind the forced "resettlement" of Jews in Nazi Germany, or peasants in Soviet Russia and Communist China, especially because Offred says no one knows what happens to these people after they move. Atwood implies that Gilead has revived the racist ideology of the past to separate the races once and for all.

The Ceremony reveals more of Gilead's connection to our world and our history. The decorations in the living room where the Bible reading takes place—paintings of women with pinched faces, constricted breasts, and stiff mouths and backs—emphasize Gilead's attempt to restore a pre-feminist world. The Bible reading itself involves the citation of an ancient authority to justify the use of Handmaids. The Handmaid-Commander relationship is intended as a response to the emergency caused by low fertility rates, but Gilead does not justify it on those grounds. Instead, Gilead's leaders claim that it is part of a biblically sanctioned tradition. Again, Atwood implies that nothing about Gilead is new; it merely takes threads from our world and weaves a new, oppressive tapestry out of them.

CHAPTERS 16–21

SUMMARY: CHAPTER 16
After the prayers and Bible reading, the Ceremony continues as usual. In the bedroom, Offred lies on her back between Serena's legs, her head resting on Serena's pubic bone. Serena is fully clothed, while Offred's skirt is hiked up and her underwear is off. The two women hold hands, and Serena's rings dig into Offred's fingers. The Commander has sex with Offred in a brisk, impersonal fashion, then zips himself up and leaves the room promptly. Serena orders Offred to leave, even though Offred is supposed to rest for ten minutes to improve her chances of getting pregnant.

SUMMARY: CHAPTER 17
Once Offred is safely alone in her bedroom, she removes the butter from her shoe and uses it as lotion for her skin because lotion and beauty products are forbidden to the Handmaids. Offred cannot sleep, so she decides to steal something. She sneaks downstairs and decides to take a daffodil from a flower arrangement. She wants to press it under her mattress and leave it for the next Handmaid to find. As she stands in the sitting room, she senses the presence of someone behind her in the room. It is Nick. Neither of them are supposed to be downstairs. Wordlessly, they kiss, and she longs to have sex with him right there. She thinks of Luke, telling him he would understand, then thinking he wouldn't. Sex is too dangerous, and Nick and Offred separate. Nick whispers that the Commander sent him to find her. The Commander wants to see her in his office tomorrow.

SUMMARY: CHAPTER 18

After returning to her room, Offred lies in her bed, remembering making love to Luke while her baby kicked inside her womb. She imagines Luke dead, his body lying in the thickets where they were caught trying to escape. She imagines that he is in prison. She also imagines that he made it safely across the border and that one day a message from him will come to her in some unexpected way. She believes in these three scenarios simultaneously, so that nothing will surprise her.

SUMMARY: CHAPTER 19

Offred dreams of catching her daughter in a hug, but a wave of sorrow overtakes her because she knows that she is dreaming. She dreams of waking up to her mother carrying in a tray a food and taking care of her. At breakfast, Offred contemplates the beauty of a boiled egg in sunlight. The sound of sirens interrupt her breakfast; it is a Birthmobile, coming to collect Offred and take her to a birth. Janine, now known as Ofwarren, is about to have her baby.

During the ride to Commander Warren's house, Offred wonders if Janine will give birth to a deformed child, an Unbaby. One in four women have been poisoned by toxins and other environmental pollution, which leads to birth deformities in their children. She recalls Aunt Lydia saying that women who did not want to have babies poisoned their own bodies or got their tubes tied. She calls these women Jezebels, scorners of God's gifts. In an old classroom, Aunt Lydia showed them a graph of how the birthrate had fallen over the course of history, eventually falling below the "line of replacement." Aunt Lydia said that women who did not want to breed were lazy sluts. She explains how much better childbirth is in Gilead in contrast to the old days, because birth is entirely natural. Women are not even allowed drugs to soothe their pain, because it is better for the baby, and because God wants women to suffer during childbirth.

The Birthmobile arrives at the home of Ofwarren's Commander, and the Handmaids file in. Then another Birthmobile pulls up, the one that carries the Wives. Offred imagines the Wives sitting around and talking about their Handmaids, calling them sluts, complaining about how unclean they are.

SUMMARY: CHAPTER 20

While Ofwarren gives birth, the Wife lies in the sitting room as if she is giving birth. Janine lies in the master bedroom, and the Handmaids gather around the bed to watch. Offred remembers how the Aunts used to show the Handmaids pornographic movies in which men practiced violent sex on women. Aunt Lydia said that was how men thought of women in the old days. One movie was about "Unwomen," feminists from the days before Gilead. The Aunts did not play the soundtrack, because they did not want the Handmaids to hear what the women said. In one of these movies, Offred saw her mother as a young woman, marching in a feminist rally. Her mother gave birth to Offred in her late thirties and chose to be a single mother. Offred and her mother used to fight, because her mother thought Offred did not appreciate the sacrifices early feminists made in order to help the next generation of women. Offred wishes she could have her mother back, fights and all.

SUMMARY: CHAPTER 21

The Handmaids chant to help Janine give birth. One Handmaid asks Offred if she is looking for someone. Offred describes Moira, and the woman tells her she will keep an eye out for a woman of that description. The woman is looking for someone named Alma. She asks Offred what her real name is, but before Offred can reply, their conversation is cut short by a suspicious glance from an Aunt who heard the break in the chant. Just before the child is born, Janine (Ofwarren) and the Wife of Warren sit on the Birthing Stool together. The Wife sits above Janine. The baby is born: a girl with no visible defects. Everyone rejoices. The Wife climbs into bed, and the baby is given to her. The other Wives crowd around, pushing the Handmaids aside, and the Wife announces she will name the baby Angela. After the birth, Janine will nurse the baby for a few months, and then she will transfer to a new Commander. Since she has produced a child, she will never be declared an Unwoman and sent to the colonies.

ANALYSIS: CHAPTERS 16–21

Offred's description of the Ceremony is supposed to be ironic, horrifying, and funny at the same time. For all the elaborate ceremonial preparations and the symbolic positioning of the bodies of Serena and Offred, the mechanical act itself makes the solemnity seem ridiculous. Offred, searching for the best word, defines the Ceremony as fucking rather than sex. She cannot call it making love or copulating, because that would imply that she enjoyed or took part in the act. And she cannot call it rape, she explains, because she was given a choice and she chose to be a Handmaid. The Commander has sex as if performing a slightly boring duty; Offred must grit her teeth and detach herself from the situation; Serena Joy, angered, grips Offred so hard that her rings cut into Offred's hand. This sex is so scripted, formal, and anonymous that no one takes any pleasure in it. Offred says sex now is simply for the purpose of reproduction, and nothing more.

The hustle and bustle surrounding Ofwarren's labor reinforces the importance of pregnancy in Gilead. Birth, now a rare event, has become a joyful community gathering for the women. However, this joy is tempered by the fear of giving birth to a deformed or defective infant—a frequent outcome as a result of widespread pollution. These deformed infants are called "Unbabies," a name that suggests society does not consider them humans. Those who do not fit into the Gileadean worldview are considered not merely dangerous or evil but actually non-human. Significantly, the "un" prefix is also attached to former feminists, called "Unwomen," who are sent to Gilead's feared Colonies. Atwood associates Giledeans with Joseph Stalin and Hitler, who dehumanized middle-class peasants and Jews in order to justify killing them. Language, in a totalitarian state, is a useful tool of oppression.

Aunt Lydia demonstrates how the patriarchal structure of Giliad borrows from and perverts the ideas of the women's movement. She tells the women of their terrible plight in the old world, when men thought of women as sex objects or as ready victims of sexual violence. Some feminists do oppose pornographic films on these grounds, saying that the films objectify women and glorify violence against women. They say pornographic films, like domestic and sexual violence of all kinds, stem from the legacy of patriarchal oppression. Aunt Lydia and Gilead agree with this condemnation of sexual violence against women, but, in contrast to the feminists, they think a patriarchal society can effectively protect women from violence. They seem to have a valid point: in Gilead, women are not judged by their bodies, catcalled, or attacked. But this safety comes at a price. Women may not be raped by strangers in Gilead, but they must submit to state-sanctioned rape by the Commanders. Sexual love and romantic love do not exist for them. And the price of this safety is the total forfeit of control over their bodies.

CHAPTERS 22–25

SUMMARY: CHAPTER 22

Driving back from the birth, Offred remembers Moira's escape from the Red Center. Moira caused a toilet to overflow, and while Aunt Elizabeth tried to fix it, Moira jabbed a metal object into Aunt Elizabeth's ribs and forced her into the furnace room. The object was a long lever from the toilet, but Aunt Elizabeth thought it was a knife. After exchanging clothing with Aunt Elizabeth and tying her up, Moira boldly walked out of the center using Aunt Elizabeth's pass. No one has seen Moira or heard from her since then.

SUMMARY: CHAPTER 23

At home, Offred tells Cora about the child, and the Martha expresses her hope that "they" (meaning Offred) will have a child soon. That night, Offred sneaks out of her room and meets the Commander in his office. She braces herself for a forced physical advance. If Serena were to discover that Offred was with the Commander in his study, she could be sent to the Colonies as an Unwoman. But if she were to refuse the Commander, there could be even more dire consequences, because he has the real power in the household. Offred eyes the walls of the study, which are filled with books. The Commander greets her in the old way, by saying "Hello," and Offred doesn't know how to reply. To her surprise, the Commander merely asks her to play a game of Scrabble. This is forbidden, since any kind of reading is forbidden to women. They play two games, and the game feels luxurious to Offred. As she is about to leave, the Commander asks her for a kiss. She imagines coming to his study again with a piece of metal from the toilet, as Moira did, putting her arms around him and killing him. She kisses him, and he says sadly he wanted her to kiss him "'as if [she] meant it.'"

SUMMARY: CHAPTER 24

> *How easy it is to invent a humanity, for anyone at all.*
> *What an available temptation.*
>
> (See QUOTATIONS, p. 70)

After leaving the Commander and returning to her room, Offred decides she has to forget her old name and her past; she needs to live in the present and work within its rules. The Commander's unorthodox behavior allows her a chance to get something from him. She remembers that underneath all of Aunt Lydia's speeches, the real message seemed to be that men are "sex machines" and should be manipulated with sex.

Offred recalls a documentary about the Holocaust in which the former mistress of one of the Nazi guards was interviewed. Offred's mother liked to watch such historical programs, and always explained them carefully to Offred, even when she was too young to understand. The guard's mistress denied knowing about the death camps and maintained that the guard, her lover, was not a monster. Offred remembers that the woman committed suicide just days after the interview.

Suddenly, sitting on her bed and undressing, Offred finds the events of the night incredibly funny. Laughter threatens to erupt, and she struggles to keep it down. In the dark, she stumbles into the closet (she also calls it a cupboard), where the Latin phrase *nolite te bastardes carborundorum* is written. She falls asleep on the floor with her head resting in the closet.

SUMMARY: CHAPTER 25

In the morning, Cora finds Offred sleeping on the floor, and she screams and drops the breakfast tray, shattering the dishes. Offred tells Cora she fainted. Cora covers for her and tells Rita that she dropped the tray by accident.

Spring gives way to summer, and Offred continues to meet the Commander in his office at night. They develop a system of signals so that Serena will not realize what is going on. If Nick is polishing the car hatless, or hat askew, the Commander wants Offred to come see him. Sometimes she cannot go because Serena is knitting in the sitting room. Other times, Serena goes out to visit other Wives when they are sick, or feigning illness. The Wives take turns being sick; Offred thinks it adds interest to their lives. Other women, the Marthas and the Handmaids, cannot afford to be sick, because the sick and old might be sent away to the Colonies. Offred says that she sees no old women, although no one really knows where they go.

The Commander does not make any further physical advances toward Offred. They play Scrabble, and he allows her to look at an old copy of *Vogue*. The women in the magazine remind her of princes or pirates. On the third night she asks the Commander for some hand lotion. He laughs when Offred tells him the Handmaids use butter to keep their skin moist, which infuriates her. She leaves the lotion in his office so that it will not be found in her room.

ANALYSIS: CHAPTERS 22–25

The story of Moira's escape makes her a symbol of rebellion and resistance for the Handmaids. She is the only woman in the novel who dares to resist Gilead directly. She lacks the strength of her oppressors, but she makes up for it with her resourcefulness and canniness. Her escape from the Red Center is a masterpiece of clever planning and bravado. Moira's exchange of clothing with Aunt Elizabeth is an important symbolic gesture; Gilead uses clothing to define rank, and by stealing the Aunt's high-ranking uniform, Moira strikes a blow against Gilead's attempt to define her identity.

The Commander, the only major male character in the novel, embodies Gilead's patriarchy. His character becomes fleshed out as Offred begins to visit him in his study. Her first impressions surprise us; we expect the Commander to behave cruelly, but he seems almost likable. Like the women, he seems to be a prisoner of Gilead, starved for genuine human contact. He behaves in a shy, courtly fashion around Offred, careful not to make unreasonable demands or intimidate her. He seems to want her to like him, and even to feel attracted to him, which explains his wistful disappointment at the coldness of her kiss. Offred finds herself liking him in spite of herself.

Ultimately, however, the problems of his life seem laughable compared to the problems of Offred's. Though kind, the Commander still works as an enforcer of the rules of the totalitarian state. Furthermore, it seems he has no true understanding of the plight of women. He laughs at Offred's admission that Handmaids put butter on their hands—their ingenuity pleases him. He does not understand the humiliation of these women, treated like animals or babies, forced to hide scraps of their own dinner, denied the tiniest luxuries. He does not even understand that their rooms are searched, that they live under constant scrutiny and have no privacy whatsoever. Offred's memory of the documentary about the Nazi guard and his mistress creates an obvious parallel to her situation with the Commander. The Commander is a human being, and like all human beings he is not pure evil. But then, neither were the Nazis pure evil. "He was not a monster, to her," Offred says as she thinks of the concentration camp guard and his mistress. "Probably he had some endearing trait ... How easy it is to invent a humanity, for anyone at all." The Commander is human, even endearing, but he nevertheless bears responsibility for the monstrous world of Gilead.

CHAPTERS 26–28

SUMMARY: CHAPTER 26

Now that Offred has a friendship with the Commander, she feels embarrassed about having sex with him during the Ceremony. Offred still hates Serena, but she also feels jealous of her, and guilty, since she realizes that she is now the Commander's mistress despite the absence of any covert sexual activity between them. If Serena were to find out what was going on, she could expel Offred. Once, the Commander almost touches Offred's face during the Ceremony, and she later tells him never to touch her because Serena could transfer her to the Colonies. He says he finds sex impersonal, and she asks him how long it took him to figure that out. She is becoming more comfortable with him. Offred remembers Aunt Lydia telling the Handmaids that the population would eventually reach an acceptable level, at which point the Handmaids would live in only one household, instead of getting transferred, and Handmaids would become like daughters to the Wives.

SUMMARY: CHAPTER 27

Ofglen and Offred, now more comfortable with one another, continue to make their shopping trips. The fish store, Loaves and Fishes, rarely opens now, because the seas have become so polluted that few fish still live in them. They continue to visit the Wall, and Offred wonders if Luke is imprisoned behind the Wall in the place that used to be a university and now serves as a detention center. On one of their return trips, Ofglen and Offred stop at a store called Soul Scrolls. Inside, humming machines print prayers. Many of the Wives phone in orders for prayers in order to signal their piety. After the prayers are printed, the paper is recycled and used again.

Suddenly, Ofglen whispers to Offred, asking her whether she believes God actually listens to the machines. Ofglen's question is treasonous, but Offred decides to trust Ofglen and answers, "No." The two women realize they can trust one another. Offred is tremendously excited. She learns that Ofglen is part of a group of subversives. As they walk home, a dark black van painted with a white-winged eye, the symbol of the Eyes, stops abruptly. Offred thinks perhaps her conversation with Ofglen was recorded, but the two Eyes who jump out grab a man carrying a briefcase. They drag him into the vehicle and drive away, and Offred feels tremendous relief.

SUMMARY: CHAPTER 28

Offred recalls how Moira disapproved of her affair with Luke, saying that Offred was poaching on another woman's property. We learn that Moira was a lesbian. Offred accused Moira of poaching women, and Moira says it is different with women. It is hot in Offred's room, and she has been given a fan. She muses that if she were Moira, she would know how to take the fan apart and use the blades as a weapon. She thinks of how strange it now seems to her that women used to have jobs.

Offred remembers the fall of the United States and the creation of Gilead. First, the president was shot and Congress was machine-gunned; then the army declared a state of emergency, telling everyone to remain calm. Islamic fanatics were falsely blamed for the execution of the entire government. The Constitution was suspended. In shock, people stayed at home and watched their televisions. At this point, Moira warned Offred that something terrible was going to happen. Slowly, the newspapers were censored and roadblocks appeared, and soon everyone had to carry an Identipass. There was a crackdown on smut of all kinds: the "Pornomarts" shut down, and the "Feels-on-Wheels vans" and "Bun-dle Buggies" disappeared.

In Offred's pre-Gilead days, paper money had been replaced by Compucards that accessed bank accounts directly. One day after the fall of the government, Offred tried to use her Compucard in the local store, and her number was declared invalid. She went to her job at the library, phoned her bank, and got a recording stating that the lines were overloaded. Later that afternoon, her boss appeared looking disheveled and distraught. He told Offred and her female coworkers that he had to fire them, because it was the law. The women had to leave within ten minutes. Two men wearing army uniforms and carrying machine guns watched over the procedure.

When she reached her home, Offred called Moira and learned that women could no longer legally work or hold property. Their bank accounts were transferred to their husbands or the nearest male family member. Luke tried to console her, but Offred wondered if he was already patronizing her. She realizes that the army men she saw were not members of the United States army. They were wearing different uniforms. In the weeks and months that fol-

THE HANDMAID'S TALE 🍁 47

lowed, there were protests and marches, but the army cracked down hard on dissent and the protesting stopped. Offred and Luke never joined any of the protests, because they were afraid for their lives and for the life of their daughter. Remembering the marches makes Offred remember earlier protests in which her mother was involved. She remembers being an adolescent and being ashamed of her mother's activism.

Looking out her window, Offred sees Nick come into the yard and notices that his hat is askew. She wonders, idly, what he gets out of facilitating her forbidden liaisons with the Commander, and she remembers their fleeting kiss in the darkened living room. Then she remembers how the night after she lost her job, Luke wanted to make love, but Offred felt uncomfortable, because the balance of power had shifted subtly. They no longer belonged to each other; instead, she belonged to him. She thought perhaps he liked the fact that she belonged to him. Now she wants to know whether she was right.

ANALYSIS: CHAPTERS 26–28

Ofglen provides Offred with hope. She is a friend with whom she can talk and a connection to the resistance movement. Atwood juxtaposes Offred's sudden sense of hope with an immediate reminder of the power of the Gileadean state: the two Handmaids witness the Eyes seize a man and drag him off. Against this display of the state's reach, the idea of a resistance seems laughable.

Offred's extended flashback provides an explanation of how Gilead was created. The pre-Gilead United States is our world in the near future—all money has been computerized, and pornography and prostitution have become more accepted and available. Offred mentions "Pornomarts" and "Feels-on-Wheels" as if the terms needed no explanation, leaving the details to the imagination but conveying a sense of a society more sexually liberated than our own. The extent of this sexual liberation may prompt the extremism of the conservative backlash. Offred mentions "porn riots" and "abortion riots" that take place before Gilead—the conservative precursor to the uprising against the liberal government. In the epilogue, an expert on Gilead's history says its founders used a "CIA pamphlet on the destabilization of foreign governments as a strategic handbook" to topple the U.S. government. First, governmental officials are assassinated; then martial law is declared "temporarily"; finally, the new regime consolidates its power and squashes dissent.

In Offred's telling, there is little resistance to the new regime, even after it disenfranchises women and strips them of their jobs. This may be intended as a condemnation of the complacency of ordinary people in times of crisis, or of the complacency Atwood saw at the time she wrote the novel. Pre-Gilead society seems more fraught with gender tensions, and these may play a role in the strange reaction of the women. When Offred loses her job and her money, Luke does not express outrage; he tells her not to worry and promises to take care of her. Later, during marches, he tells her that it would be "futile" to march and that she needs to think about him and their daughter. Everything we know of Luke suggests that he is a decent man, but he is willing to go along with this oppression of women. Gilead re-establishes the old patterns of patriarchy, and Luke slips back into those patterns, promising to "take care" of Offred instead of fighting for her rights. Women also bear blame: they do not respond to the outrages against feminism with rage or action, but with lassitude. Offred doesn't know or remember the details of the coup. This ignorance, in her and in other women, may have been the failure. Women took for granted the gains of feminism and the government's protection of the rights of women, and so lost them all.

CHAPTERS 29–32

SUMMARY: CHAPTER 29

The Commander and Offred have become more informal with one another. After a game of Scrabble, he offers her a magazine as usual, but she wants to talk instead. She tries to get information about him, but he gives her vague answers. Then she asks him what the Latin phrase in her room means. The Commander translates it as "don't let the bastards grind you down," and explains that the phrase is a schoolboy joke. Offred guesses that the former Handmaid must have learned the phrase from him and scratched it into the floor. She asks what happened to that Handmaid. The Commander replies that Serena discovered their nighttime liaisons, and the Handmaid hanged herself. Suddenly, Offred realizes that the Commander summons her to his office because he wants her life to be bearable: he feels guilty. She knows that his guilt is a weapon she can use. The Commander asks her what would make her life better. Offred asks for knowledge about "what's going on."

SUMMARY: CHAPTER 30

Later that night, Offred stares through her window and catches sight of Nick. She senses the charge of sexual desire in the glance they exchange before she pulls the curtains closed. She remembers the day she and Luke tried to escape from Gilead. They did not pack anything because they did not want to look as if they were leaving permanently. Luke killed their pet cat because they did not want to leave her to starve, and leaving her to meow outside would arouse suspicion. Someone must have reported their plans, because the escape attempt failed. It could have been a neighbor or the man who forged their passports. Offred wonders if the Eyes sometimes posed as forgers in order to catch people trying to escape. Lying in the dark, she prays in a confused fashion and thinks about suicide.

SUMMARY: CHAPTER 31

Summer drags on—with no hope of release from the horror of life in Gilead, the passage of time is unbearable. During a shopping trip one day, Ofglen and Offred find two new bodies on the Wall. One is a Catholic, and another is marked with J, which the women do not understand. If he were Jewish, he would be marked with a yellow star. In the early days of Gilead, Jews were accorded special status as "Sons of Jacob," and they had the choice of converting or emigrating to Israel. Some people pretended to be Jewish and escaped Gilead that way. Many Jews left, but others pretended to convert or refused to convert; now those who did not truly convert are hanged when caught.

Ofglen tells Offred that subversives in Gilead use "mayday" as a password, but she warns Offred not to use it often. If she is caught and tortured, she should not know names of other subversives. When Offred reaches the house, she notes that Nick's hat is askew. Serena calls Offred over and asks her to hold the wool while she knits. She asks if there is any sign of pregnancy. When Offred indicates there is not, Serena suggests that the Commander may be sterile. After a moment of hesitation, Offred agrees that it is possible. Serena suggests she try another man, since Offred's time is running out. Serena says Nick would be the safest possibility, and then offers to let Offred see a picture of her daughter if she agrees. Blinded by sudden hate for Serena, Offred nonetheless agrees, and Serena gives her a cigarette as a reward and instructs her to ask Rita for a match.

SUMMARY: CHAPTER 32

> *The problem wasn't only with the women, he says.*
> *The main problem was with the men. There was*
> *nothing for them anymore.* (See QUOTATIONS, p. 71)

Offred considers eating the cigarette little by little for the nicotine rush and saving the match to burn down the house. The Commander has taken to drinking during his evenings with Offred. Ofglen says Offred's Commander is high in the chain of power. One night he explains that in the old world, before Gilead, there was nothing for men to do with women anymore—nothing to struggle for, nothing to hold their interest. Men used to complain that they felt nothing. He asks what she thinks of Gilead. Offred tries to empty her mind; she cannot give her real opinion. She does not answer, but he can feel her unhappiness. "You can't make an omelette without breaking eggs," he says. "We thought we could do better."

ANALYSIS: CHAPTERS 29–32

Even before she knew what it meant, Offred cherished the Latin scrawl *nolites te bastardes carborundorum* as a connection between her and the previous Handmaid, and as a symbol of her resistance to Gilead. Now, thanks to the Commander, she learns that it means "don't let the bastards grind you down"—an appropriate response to a totalitarian, patriarchal society. Offred and the other Handmaids must struggle to hold on to their humanity, and to resist their oppressors. The translation of the phrase is not an entirely joyous moment, however, for it signals to Offred that someone came to the Commander's study before her. It is not clear whether this upsets her because she feels jealous of her connection with the Commander, or because she worries about the fate of the Handmaid before her.

The Commander's comments and revelations during his evenings with Offred cast him in an increasingly unflattering light. His admission that the previous Handmaid also made forbidden, clandestine visits to his study, and that she hanged herself after Serena found out, makes him seem selfish and obtuse. He not only evinces no concern over the suicide of the Handmaid; he seems unfazed by the possibility that Serena might discover Offred's visits too. He recognizes that he is putting Offred's position and possibly her life at risk in order to satisfy his desire for a little bit of intimacy, but he does not seem to care.

The Commander's explanation of the reasoning employed by the founders of Gilead shows the founders to be equally selfish. He tells Offred that men in the old world found everything too easy, too available—especially women and sex. Gilead, from the Commander's point of view, has restored meaning to men's lives. He insists that it has made them "feel" again. Yet he does not realize that such feeling comes at the price of human misery, which is borne by the women of Gilead. When Offred wonders how he can imagine Gilead to be better than the old world, the Commander callously replies that "[b]etter . . . always means worse, for some." The Commander thinks he has made men happier and more fulfilled. If that means that life is ghastly and oppressive for women, so be it.

While the Commander looks colder and crueler in these chapters, Serena Joy briefly comes across as, if not kind, then at least willing to consider Offred a fellow human being. Serena's suggestion that her husband is sterile establishes a brief moment of unity between the two women, against the Commander and the other men of Gildead, who refuse to acknowledge that men can be sterile. Yet Serena's offer to help Offred get pregnant, even though it is a kind request because it will keep Offred from the Colonies, is also a selfish one, since it is Serena and not Offred who will raise the child. And Serena's offer to get a photo of Offred's daughter reveals that Serena has known where the girl is all along but has never mentioned her or given Offred news of her. Again, the cruelty of women to other women in Gilead proves as bad as, if not worse than, anything the men inflict on women.

The trip to the Wall creates an explicit parallel between Gilead and Nazi Germany. We have already seen that Gilead, like the Nazis, persecutes Catholics, executes homosexuals ("gender traitors"), and practices racism; now we see that it is anti-Semitic as well. Offred describes Gilead's anti-Jewish laws, which provide for deportation, and then create an Inquisition-style atmosphere for those who remain and do not convert.

CHAPTERS 33–36

SUMMARY: CHAPTER 33

Ofglen and Offred attend a "Prayvaganza" with the other women of their district, held in what used to be a university building. The Wives sit in one section with their daughters, the Marthas and

Econowives sit in another, and the Handmaids kneel in a section cordoned off by ropes. Janine walks in with a new Wife, and Ofglen whispers that Janine's baby was deformed, a "shredder" after all. She adds that Janine slept with a doctor to get pregnant. Offred remembers a strange episode in the Red Center when Janine sat on her bed staring off into space, speaking to an invisible customer in a restaurant where she worked before Gilead. Moira slapped Janine and shouted until Janine came back to her senses.

SUMMARY: CHAPTER 34
Women's Prayvaganzas are weddings for the Wives' daughters, mass ceremonies in which girls as young as fourteen get married. In a few years, the brides will be girls who do not remember life before Gilead. Offred remembers a conversation with the Commander, in which he insisted that while Gilead has taken away some freedom, it has guaranteed women safety and dignity. Now all women have spouses, and they are not left alone to care for children, beaten, or forced to work if they do not want to. They can "fulfill their biological destinies in peace." Offred noted that they do not allow love, but the Commander replied that arranged marriages work better than falling in love.

Although women's Prayvaganzas usually celebrate group weddings and men's celebrate military victories, sometimes the Prayvaganzas celebrate Catholic nuns who convert to the state religion. When the authorities of Gilead catches Catholic nuns, they torture them. They send old ones directly to the Colonies, but young ones may choose between the Colonies and conversion. If they convert, the nuns become Handmaids, but many choose the Colonies.

The wedding ceremony goes on, and Offred remembers how Aunt Lydia always said that the real goal of Gilead is to create camaraderie between women. After the services, Ofglen whispers that the subversives know she sees the Commander in private. She urges Offred to find out everything she can.

SUMMARY: CHAPTER 35
Offred's thoughts return, against her will, to the day she and Luke tried to escape Gilead. They reached the border and gave the guard their passports, which said that Luke had never been divorced. Luke saw the guard pick up the phone. They sped away in the car, and then got out and tried to run through the woods. Offred shakes off these memories and tries to remember love and how it

felt to be in love—how hard it was, and how precious, and how people defined their lives around it. Thinking that Luke must be dead, she begins to cry. Later that night, Serena shows Offred a photograph of her daughter. In the photo, she wears a white dress and smiles. Offred senses that her daughter hardly remembers her. This tears at her heart.

SUMMARY: CHAPTER 36

When Offred goes to see the Commander that night, he seems drunk. He speaks playfully with her and gives her a skimpy outfit decorated with feathers and sequins. He wants to take her out, he claims, using an expression from pre-Gilead days; she agrees to go. She dons the costume and puts cheap makeup on her face. She wears one of Serena's blue winter cloaks when he escorts her out of the house. Nick is waiting for them in the car, and they drive through darkened city streets. Offred hides on the floor when they pass the gateway. Offred finds herself worrying about Nick's opinion of her. The car stops in an alley, and the Commander helps Offred out of the robe. He opens a door with a key and slips a purple tag around Offred's wrist, instructing her to tell anyone who asks that she is an "evening rental." As Offred enters the building, she imagines Moira calling her an idiot for going along with this.

ANALYSIS: CHAPTERS 33—36

The word Prayvaganza combines "pray" with "extravaganza," and emphasizes that in the new order, prayer serves a public, state function. Church and state, far from being separated, make up one entity. Prayer is no longer a private matter, but a public spectacle and an act of patriotic fervor. The banner that hangs over the Prayvaganza sums up the new church-state relationship. It reads "God is a National Resource."

When the Commander justifies the marriage process in Gilead, he offers a compelling critique of the old order (and consequently of our society). Again using feminist rhetoric, he makes several valid points: society should not force women to spend their entire paycheck on day care, it should value the work of mothering, it should not allow fathers to run off and abandon children, it should not allow domestic abuse. In Gilead, none of these conditions officially exist. Still, Offred deflates the Commander's argument by pointing out the importance of love. She points out that such a scheme, while removing some uncertainty and unhappiness, leaves out the possibility of freedom. Arranged marriages are, by definition, the opposite of free choice. Romance, though uncertain, is an ultimate expression of the soul's liberty, the liberty to choose whom to love.

The Commander comments in Chapter 32 that men could not feel before Gilead, but it seems that for Offred, Gilead erases the ability to feel. In depriving her and other women of the opportunity to be in love, Gilead amputates their ability to feel. After the Prayvaganza, Offred thinks of how love felt and is overcome by a wave of strong emotion. She can only cling to her memories of Luke and what loving him felt like. She reflects that the next generation will have no such memories. This affirms Aunt Lydia's sinister comment that Gildead will eventually "become ordinary." Atwood suggests that this closing of the horizon is the dark power of a totalitarian society. Once people cannot imagine anything other than oppression, oppression becomes ordinary.

Atwood draws a parallel between the nuns forced to become Handmaids and the Handmaids themselves. The Handmaids resemble nuns: both groups are cloistered, consecrated to a religious duty, and required to wear long garments referred to as "habits." But whereas nuns vow to remain celibate and serve God by ignoring their fertility and their sexual urges, Handmaids' sole religious and social duty is to reproduce. According to the worldview of Gilead, nuns pose a greater threat to the totalitarian order than divorced women or women who have premarital sex. The women in the latter groups are simply behaving immorally, but the nuns are taking themselves out of the sexual world entirely. Since Gilead is built on sexual control, the adoption of a celibate life is the ultimate rejection of the totalitarian order.

CHAPTERS 37–40

SUMMARY: CHAPTER 37

The Commander takes Offred to an old hotel that Offred remembers from pre-Gilead days, when she often met Luke there. In the central courtyard, Offred sees women dressed in gaudy and revealing clothing from the past. The women mingle with important, powerful men. Offred realizes she should stay quiet and look dumb. She senses that the Commander likes showing her off and enjoys showing off for her. He explains that "the club" is officially forbid-

den, but that everyone knows that to be satisfied, men require a variety of women. Some of the women were prostitutes before Gilead. Others, once lawyers, sociologists, and businesswomen, prefer turning tricks in the club to a life in the Colonies or as a Handmaid. Suddenly Offred spots Moira in the crowd. Moira wears an ill-fitting Playboy bunny costume. She turns and sees Offred. They pretend not to recognize one another, and then Moira gives the old signal to meet her in the washroom.

SUMMARY: CHAPTER 38

Five minutes later, Offred makes her way to the washroom. A dressed-up Aunt standing guard with a cattle prod tells her she has fifteen minutes. Offred meets Moira inside and explains that the Commander smuggled her into the club just for the night. Moira tells her own story. After escaping from the Red Center, she made her way to the center of town in Aunt Elizabeth's clothes and went to the home of a Quaker couple involved in the resistance. She says at that time the general public did not know about the Red Center because the authorities of Gilead feared people would object at first. The Quakers put her on the Underground Femaleroad, a system for getting women to safety. They tried to smuggle her out of the country, but just as Moira was leaving the final safe house to slip across the border in a boat, she was caught. The Eyes tortured her and showed her movies of the Colonies, where old women and subversives clean up radioactive spills and dead bodies from the war, and the life expectancy is three years. Moira chose to work as a prostitute in the club, which is nicknamed "Jezebel's," rather than go to the Colonies. Offred is disappointed to hear the fatalism in Moira's voice—Moira resignedly tells Offred she should try to work at the club, where they get three or four years to live, and face cream. Offred misses the old Moira who was so spirited and full of rebellion. After she leaves the club, she never sees Moira again.

SUMMARY: CHAPTER 39

The Commander takes Offred to a hotel room, which reminds her of her affair with Luke. She excuses herself to go to the bathroom. She hears toilets flushing in other rooms and feels comforted, thinking of the universality of bodily functions. She thinks about Moira and her mother. In the washroom, Moira said that she saw Offred's mother in one of the films about the Colonies. Offred had assumed her mother was dead. Offred remembers going to her mother's apartment with Luke during the early days of Gilead; she found the place in disarray and her mother gone. Luke told her not to call the police, saying it wouldn't do any good. She remembers how much spirit her mother used to have, but she realizes that the Colonies must have stripped it away. The Commander is lying on the bed waiting for her when she exits the bathroom. He seems disappointed that she is not excited about a real sexual encounter. He looks smaller and older without his clothing. Offred feels no excitement and silently orders herself to fake it.

SUMMARY: CHAPTER 40

Back in her room at the Commander's house, Offred has removed her makeup and put on her Handmaid clothes. Serena plans to meet her at midnight to take her to Nick so that Offred and Nick can have sex. In the middle of the night, Serena comes and tells Offred to go to Nick's apartment. Serena will wait for Offred to return.

Offred twice tells the story of what happens next. The first story, thick with passion and desire, is told in the breathy language of a romance novel. The second, probably more accurate, is awkward, uncertain, and full of sadness for the lost courtship rituals of the pre-Gilead world. "No romance . . . okay?" Nick says before they begin. Offred takes pleasure in the act this time. Offred says that neither of the versions is completely accurate, that every story is by nature a reconstruction. After sleeping with Nick, she feels ashamed. She feels she betrayed Luke and wonders if she would feel differently if she knew Luke was dead.

ANALYSIS: CHAPTERS 38–40

Atwood suggests that patriarchal societies tend to divide women into two types: the virgin and the whore. In Gilead, the virginal women are the nearly sexless Wives and daughters, the invisible Marthas, and the holy Handmaids—all of whose sexual lives are tightly restricted. The whores are the prostitutes at Jezebel's. Jezebel, for whom the men's club is named, was an evil Old Testament queen, guilty of every sort of depravity, who came to symbolize the prototypically vicious woman in the Judeo-Christian imagination. The men of Gilead admit to no middle ground or gray area between virgin and whore.

The club exposes the hypocrisy of the powerful men who prate about sexual morality and then spend their evenings dallying with

prostitutes. Officially, Gilead draws its ideology from the Old Testament (it warps the Old Testament in order to suit its ideas) and wholly rejects modern science. Yet to justify Jezebel's existence, the Commander snatches at the rhetoric of late-twentieth-century evolutionary psychologists, lecturing Offred on how men need multiple sexual partners because "Nature demands variety . . . it's part of the procreational strategy." The Commanders pick and choose from earlier traditions as they please. The Old Testament is useful for subjugating women, but modern sociobiology provides justification for their own philandering.

During her encounter with Moira, Offred learns that the spirit of her mother and that of Moira, both figures of transgression and resistance, have been broken. At the Red Center, Moira was an icon whose actions suggested that fighting Gilead was possible. Offred's mother, a feminist and a political activist, embodied everything that Gilead condemns. Although Offred once took for granted the freedoms her mother's generation fought for, now, trapped in Gilead, she realizes that her mother was like Moira, an embodiment of resistance to the regime. At Jezebel's, Moira says she is resigned to her fate. She seems listless and trapped. Instead of embodying defiance, Moira now embodies Gilead's ability to crush even the strongest spirit. When Offred learns that her mother went to the Colonies, she knows her mother will not have any strength left for resistance, even if she is still alive. Only one flash of hope lights up Moira's narrative: her description of the Underground Femaleroad, an underground network working to smuggle women out of Gilead. Its name references the Underground Railroad, which transported escaped slaves from safe house to safe house in the days before the Civil War in the United States. The fact that such a network exists gives us the sense that even if Moira herself has given up hope, the struggle against Gilead presses on.

Atwood juxtaposes Offred's sexual encounters with the Commander and with Nick to highlight the difference between forced sex and sex by choice. While the Commander has sex with her, Offred cannot muster any passion. Her passivity disappoints the Commander, who seems to want romance and passion despite his praise for arranged marriages. Atwood's novel suggests that Offred cannot give him passion because she sleeps with him against her will, and romance requires the exercise of free will. Because Gilead outlaws the freedom essential to passion, the Commander cannot call it into being to suit his whims. Offred and Nick's coupling, on the other hand, has a spark, a sense of desire. Offred narrates the scene in an elegiac tone, depicting her sex with Nick as an act of mourning for the vanished world of romance and courtship and love. His request, "no romance," reminds them of what they cannot have.

CHAPTERS 41–44

SUMMARY: CHAPTER 41

Offred tells her imagined listener that her story is almost too painful to bear, but that she needs to go on telling it because it wills her listener into being. She may be addressing the reader, or she may be addressing Luke; she says she wants to hear her listener's story too, if her listener escapes. Offred says she continues to see Nick at night without Serena's knowledge. She feels thankful each time he opens the door to her. He never says much, but she finds herself telling him about Moira and Ofglen. She tells him her real name. She never mentions Luke. Eventually, she tells him she thinks she is pregnant, although privately she feels this is wishful thinking. During their shopping trips, Ofglen pressures Offred to break into the Commander's office. She wants Offred to find out what he really does, what responsibilities he has. But Offred now tunes out Ofglen and spends her time thinking about Nick.

SUMMARY: CHAPTER 42

A women's "Salvaging," or large-scale execution, is held in what used to be Harvard Yard. All the women in the district must attend. On the lawn in front of the former library sits a stage like the one used for commencement in pre-Gilead days. Aunt Lydia sits on the stage, supervising the hangings. It is the first time Offred has seen Aunt Lydia since leaving the Red Center. Aunt Lydia announces that they have decided to discontinue announcing the crimes of the convicted because it sparks copycat crimes. The Handmaids are dismayed; the crimes give them hope by showing them that women can still resist. Three women are hanged, two Handmaids and one Wife. Offred speculates that the Handmaid tried to kill her Commander's Wife. She says Wives get salvaged for only three things: killing a Handmaid, adultery, or attempted escape. The Handmaids must place their hands on a long rope as the women hang, in order to show their consent to the salvaging.

SUMMARY: CHAPTER 43

After the hanging, Aunt Lydia instructs the Handmaids to form a circle. A few of the other women leave, but most Wives and daughters stay to watch. Then two Guardians drag a third Guardian to the front. He is disheveled and smells of excrement. He looks drunk or drugged. Aunt Lydia announces that he and another Guardian have been convicted of rape. His partner was shot already, but this man has been saved for the Handmaids, who will take part in what is called a "Particicution." Aunt Lydia adds that one of the two Handmaids involved was pregnant and lost the baby in the attack. A wave of raw fury courses through the crowd; Offred feels bloodlust along with the others. Aunt Lydia blows a whistle, and the Handmaids close in on the man, kicking and beating him to a bloody pulp. Ofglen dashes in first and kicks his head several times. Afterward, disgusted with her friend, Offred asks Ofglen why she did it. Ofglen whispers that the supposed rapist was part of the underground rebellion, and she wanted to put him out of his misery quickly. Offred sees Janine carrying a bloody clump of hair. Her eyes look vacant, and she babbles some cheerful greetings from the time before Gilead. Offred admits, ashamed, that she feels great hunger.

SUMMARY: CHAPTER 44

Soon after the Salvaging, Offred goes out for a shopping trip, comforted by the ordinariness of the routine. To her dismay, the Handmaid who meets her is not Ofglen. When Offred asks her where Ofglen went, the woman replies, "I am Ofglen." Since this new Handmaid now lives with the Commander named Glen, her name becomes Ofglen. Offred realizes how women get lost in this ocean of fluctuating names. Trying to see if the new woman belongs to the resistance, Offred suggests they go to the Wall. As they walk there, Offred works the password "Mayday" into the conversation by mentioning the old holiday of "May Day." The new Ofglen looks at her coolly and tells her that she should forget such "echoes" from the old world. Terrified, Offred realizes that the new Ofglen knows about the resistance and does not belong to it. She suddenly imagines herself found out and arrested. She thinks that perhaps they will torture her daughter until she tells them everything she knows. She and the new, treacherous Ofglen walk home. As they part, the new Ofglen suddenly whispers that the old Ofglen hanged herself when she saw the van coming to arrest her. "'It was better,'" she says, and then walks quickly away.

ANALYSIS: CHAPTERS 41–44

As soon as she begins her affair with Nick, Offred slips into complacency, showing how it is that oppressive regimes like Gilead come to power and survive unchallenged when their subjects become listless. Offred remembers her mother saying that people can grow accustomed to almost anything "as long as there are a few compensations," and Offred's relationship with Nick shows the truth of this insight. Offred's situation restricts her horribly compared to the freedom her former life allowed, but her relationship with Nick allows her to reclaim the tiniest fragment of her former existence. The physical affection and companionship becomes a compensation that makes the restrictions almost bearable. Offred seems suddenly so content that the idea of change, embodied in the demands that Ofglen makes of her, becomes too difficult to contemplate. The Salvaging shakes Offred, however, and her complacency shatters when Ofglen disappears and a sinister, conformist woman takes her place. During this climactic shopping trip, the horror of living in a totalitarian state reasserts itself, and events begin to rush toward the novel's conclusion.

The "Salvaging" and its aftermath show Gilead at its most cruel. It is unclear why the execution is called a salvaging, a word that means "saving." Perhaps the name refers to the society at large, which is saved from the potential threat posed by the offenders when those offenders are hanged. Less ambiguous is the meaning of the "particicution," a term derived by combining the words "participation" and "execution." As its etymology suggests, the particicution is an execution carried out by a group. Its design shows the cleverness of Gileadean totalitarianism, since it provides both a gruesome death for traitors and discourages other rebels, who face the possibility of dying at the hands of those they were trying to help. Its main function, though, is to provide an outlet for the rage and hatred that the Handmaids harbor toward the men who oppress them. Even before Aunt Lydia announces the guilty Guardian's crime, a "murmur of readiness and anger" builds among the Handmaids. They burst with frustration and anger at their repressed existence, and perhaps at their inability to conceive children. Without outlets for women's emotions, Gilead faces the danger of a sudden upheaval. By allowing them to participate in the Guardian's execution, Gilead channels the Handmaids' anger onto a single man, who serves as a scapegoat for everyone else. The man is presented as a rapist of Handmaids who caused a miscarriage, meaning that not only does he suggest the sanctioned rape of the Handmaids by the Commanders, but he has robbed the women of the one thing that gives them value, babies.

The Salvaging takes place in Harvard Yard, in front of what was Widener Library. As a university, Harvard once symbolized the free pursuit of knowledge; as the location for the Salvaging, it symbolizes the denial of access to knowledge. Gilead has turned the old world upside down, making a former liberal arts university the seat of the secret police.

CHAPTERS 45–46 & HISTORICAL NOTES ON *THE HANDMAID'S TALE*

SUMMARY: CHAPTER 45

Offred feels great relief when she hears that Ofglen has committed suicide, for now Ofglen will not give her name to the Eyes while being tortured. For the first time, Offred feels completely within the power of the authorities. She feels she will do anything necessary to live—stop wanting control of her body, stop resisting, stop seeing Nick. From the porch, Serena calls to Offred. When Offred comes in, she holds out her winter cloak and the sequined outfit Offred wore to the club. She asks Offred how she could be so vulgar, and then tells Offred she is a slut like the other Handmaid and will come to the same end. Nick stops whistling, but Offred does not look at him. She manages to remain calm and composed as she retreats to her room.

SUMMARY: CHAPTER 46

After her confrontation with Serena, Offred waits in her room. She feels peaceful. Night creeps in, and she wonders if she could use her hidden match and start a fire. She might die from smoke inhalation, although the fire would be subdued quickly. Or she could hang herself in her room from the hooks in the closet, she thinks. Or she could wait for Serena and kill her when she opens the door to her room. Nothing seems to matter. In the twilight, she hears the van coming for her, and she regrets not doing something while she had the chance. As the van pulls into the driveway, she sees the Eyes painted on its sides.

The van pulls in, and Nick opens the door of Offred's room. Offred thinks he has betrayed her, but he whispers that she should go with the Eyes. He tells her they are in Mayday and have come to save her. Offred knows that he might be an Eye, because the Eyes probably know all about Mayday, but this is her last chance. She walks down the stairs to meet the men waiting for her. Serena demands to know Offred's crime, and Offred realizes Serena was not the one to call these men. The men say they cannot tell her. The Commander demands to see a warrant, and the Eyes—or the men from Mayday, perhaps—say that she is being arrested for "violation of state secrets." As Serena curses her, Offred follows the Eyes to the van waiting outside.

Summary: Historical Notes on
The Handmaid's Tale

The epilogue is a transcript of a symposium held in 2195, in a university in the Arctic. Gilead is long gone, and Offred's story has been published as a manuscript titled The Handmaid's Tale. Her story was found recorded on a set of cassette tapes locked in an army foot locker in Bangor, Maine. The main part of the epilogue is a speech by an expert on Gilead named Professor Pieixoto. He talks about authenticating the cassette tapes. He says tapes like these would be very difficult to fake. The first section of each tape contains a few songs from the pre-Gileadean period, probably to camouflage the actual purpose of the tapes. The same voice speaks on all the tapes, and they are not numbered, nor are they arranged in any particular order, so the professors who transcribed the story had to guess at the intended chronology of the tapes.

Pieixoto warns his audience against judging Gilead too harshly, because such judgments are culturally biased, and he points out that the Gilead regime was under a good deal of pressure from the falling birthrate and environmental degradation. He says the birthrate declined for a variety of reasons, including birth control, abortions, AIDS, syphilis, and deformities and miscarriages resulting from nuclear plant disasters and toxic waste. The professor explains how Gilead created a group of fertile women by criminalizing all second marriages and nonmarital relationships, confiscating children of those marriages and partnerships, and using the women as reproductive vessels. Using the Bible as justification, they replaced what he calls "serial polygamy" with "simultaneous polygamy." He explains that like all new systems, Gilead drew on the past in creating its ideology. In particular, he mentions the racial tensions that plagued pre-Gilead, which Gilead incorporated in its doctrine.

He discusses the identity of the narrator. They tried to discover it using a variety of methods, but failed. Pieixoto notes that historical details are scanty because so many records were destroyed in purges and civil war. Some tapes, however, were smuggled to Save the Women societies in England. He says the names Offred used to describe her relatives were likely pseudonyms employed to protect the identities of her loved ones. The Commander was likely either Frederick Waterford or B. Frederick Judd. Both men were leaders in the early years of Gilead, and both were probably instrumental in building the society's basic structure. Judd devised the Particicution, realizing that it would release the pent-up anger of the Handmaids. Pieixoto says that Particicutions became so popular that in Gilead's "Middle Period" they occurred four times a year. Judd also came up with the notion that women should control other women. Pieixoto says that no empire lacks this "control of the indigenous by members of their own group." Pieixoto explains that both Waterford and Judd likely came into contact with a virus that caused sterility in men. He says the evidence suggests that Waterford was the Commander of Offred's story; records show that in "one of the earliest purges" Waterford was killed for owning pictures and books, and for indulging "liberal tendencies." Pieixoto remarks that many early Commanders felt themselves above the rules, safe from any attack, and that in the Middle Period Commanders behaved more cautiously.

The professor says the final fate of Offred is unknown. She may have been recaptured. If she escaped to England or Canada, it is puzzling that she did not make her story public, as many women did. However, she might have wanted to protect others who were left behind, or she may have feared repercussions against her family. Punishing the relatives of escaped Handmaids was done secretly to minimize bad publicity in foreign lands. He says Nick's motivation cannot be understood fully; he reveals that Nick was a member both of the Eyes and of Mayday, and that the men he called were sent to rescue Offred. In the end, Pieixoto says, they will probably never know the real ending of Offred's story. The novel ends with the line, "'Are there any questions?'"

ANALYSIS: CHAPTERS 45–46 &
HISTORICAL NOTES ON *THE HANDMAID'S TALE*
Offred's story ends abruptly and uncertainly, which illustrates the precarious nature of existence in a totalitarian society in which

everyone stands constantly poised on the edge of arrest and execution. Offred learns of Ofglen's death, finds that Serena knows of her
visits to Jezebel's, and is (possibly) rescued by Nick's intervention,
all in the same day. Yet, even as events move quickly, Offred herself
does absolutely nothing. Things happen to her; she does not make
them happen. She demonstrates her lack of agency when she spends
hours alone in her room, listlessly contemplating murder, suicide,
and escape, but unable to act. Gilead has stripped her of her power,
and so in a moment of crisis she can do nothing but think, and
worry, and wait for the black van to come. Throughout the novel,
Offred has maintained an internal struggle against the system, and a
cautious outward struggle. It is when the news of Ofglen's death ter-
rifies her, and when she realizes she would rather give in than die,
that help arrives. Atwood suggests that in Gilead the tiny rebellions
or resistances of one person do not necessarily matter. Offred
escapes not because of her resistance, but despite her passivity. Luck
saves her; she does not save herself.

When the van comes, Offred has no way of knowing whether it
comes to save her or to bring her to her death, but she must go. In
Gilead, women cannot escape alone. Someone must help them
attain freedom. Her story ends either in "darkness" or "light," she
says, not knowing which it will be. After this ending, with its leap
into the unknown, the epilogue follows. It is simultaneously a welcome objective explication of Gileadean society, a parody of academic conferences, and offensive to the reader. We have just
suffered through Offred's torments with her, and it is shocking, as
Atwood means it to be, to hear her life discussed in front of an
amused audience, joked about, and treated as a quaint relic.

Professor Pieixoto makes references to Gilead's clever synthesis
of ancient customs and modern beliefs, he discusses the use of biblical narratives to justify the institution of the Handmaids, and he
mentions the similarities between the "Particicution" and ancient
fertility rites. None of these things will have escaped the notice of an
alert reader, but this marks the first time we have heard them
explained clearly and analytically. The epilogue also reveals information beyond Offred's experience—the identity of Offred's Commander, the purges that took place frequently under the regime, and
the success of the underground resistance at infiltrating the com-
mand structure.

By telling us that *The Handmaid's Tale* was transcribed from
tapes found in an "Underground Femaleroad" safe house, the epi-

logue undercuts the powerful ambiguity of the novel's ending, letting us know that Nick *was* a member of Mayday, and he did attempt to get Offred out of the country. Offred's final fate remains a mystery, but the faithfulness of Nick does not.

In the epilogue, Atwood inverts Gilead, overthrowing the terrible world that she created. In opposition to the Gilead's white, male-dominated patriarchy, in the new world the whites are the subjects of study, not the scholars and rulers. Professors have names like Johnny Running Dog and Maryann Crescent Moon, which suggests that Native Americans dominate the academy. The great universities are in Nunavit, in northern Canada, and the map of the world, we are assured, has been remade. Once, white people studied the Third World; now the chair of the conference announces a speech from Professor Gopal Chatterjee, from the Department of Western Philosophy at the University of Baroda, India.

Pieixoto's comment, that Gilead should not be judged too harshly because all such judgments are culturally conditioned, echoes and calls into question the moral relativism common among academics today. The novel has asked us to sympathize with Offred, and to judge Gilead evil, tyrannical, and soul-destroying. In that case, Pieixoto's appeal for understanding, and the applause that follows it, suggests that such moral ambivalence sows seeds for future evils. The professor and the conference attendees are insufficiently moved by Offred's plight. They discuss her as a chip in a reproductive game, belittling her tale as the crumbs of history, and openly prizing a few printed pages from the Commander's computer over her tale of suffering. This belittling of a woman's life and glorification of a man's computer suggests the patriarchal leanings of this new society. Offred and her trauma are remote to this group, but Atwood's novel urges us to think that such a fate is not far off, but imaginable, for societies like ours and like Professor Pieixoto's, which fancy themselves progressive but hold seeds of patriarchal oppression. The academics' complacency and self-satisfaction seems dangerous. The closing line—"Are there any questions?"— gives the story a deliberately open-ended conclusion. The end of *The Handmaid's Tale* begins a discussion of the issues the story raises.

IMPORTANT QUOTATIONS EXPLAINED

1. Ordinary, said Aunt Lydia, is what you are used to.
    This may not seem ordinary to you now, but after a
    time it will. It will become ordinary.

This quotation is from the end of Chapter 6. Offred and Ofglen are standing by the Wall, looking at the bodies of people who have been hanged by Gilead. The sight horrifies Offred, but she strains to push aside her repugnance and substitute an emotional "blankness." As she represses her natural revulsion, she remembers Aunt Lydia's words about how life in Gilead will "become ordinary." Aunt Lydia's statement reflects the power of a totalitarian state like Gilead to transform a natural human response such as revulsion at an execution into "blankness," to transform horror into normalcy. Aunt Lydia's words suggest that Gilead succeeds not by making people believe that its ways are right, but by making people forget what a different world could be like. Torture and tyranny become accepted because they are "what you are used to."

2.   I would like to believe this is a story I'm telling. I need
     to believe it. I must believe it. Those who can believe
     that such stories are only stories have a better chance.
     If it's a story I'm telling, then I have control over the
     ending. Then there will be an ending, to the story,
     and real life will come after it. I can pick up where I
     left off.

This quotation, from the end of Chapter 7, reflects the connection
between Offred's story, her readers, her lost family, and her inner
state. These words suggest that Offred is not recounting events from
afar, looking back on an earlier period in her life. Rather, she is
describing the horror of Gilead as she experiences it from day to
day. For Offred, the act of telling her story becomes a rebellion
against her society. Gilead seeks to silence women, but Offred
speaks out, even if it is only to an imaginary reader, to Luke, or to
God. Gilead denies women control over their own lives, but
Offred's creation of a story gives her, as she puts it, "control over
the ending." Most important, Offred's creation of a narrative gives
her hope for the future, a sense that "there will be an ending . . . and
real life will come after it." She can hope that someone will hear her
story, or that she will tell it to Luke someday. Offred has found the
only avenue of rebellion available in her totalitarian society: she
denies Gilead control over her inner life.

3.   I used to think of my body as an instrument, of
      pleasure, or a means of transportation, or an
      implement for the accomplishment of my will . . .
      Now the flesh arranges itself differently. I'm a cloud,
      congealed around a central object, the shape of a pear,
      which is hard and more real than I am and glows red
      within its translucent wrapping.

This passage is from Chapter 13, when Offred sits in the bath, naked, and contrasts the way she used to think about her body to the way she thinks about it now. Before, her body was an instrument, an extension of her self; now, her self no longer matters, and her body is only important because of its "central object," her womb, which can bear a child. Offred's musings show that she has internalized Gilead's attitude toward women, which treats them not as individuals but as objects important only for the children that they can bear. Women's wombs are a "national resource," the state insists, using language that dehumanizes women and reduces them to, as Offred puts it, "a cloud, congealed around a central object, which is hard and more real than I am."

4. He was not a monster, to her. Probably he had some endearing trait: he whistled, offkey, in the shower, he had a yen for truffles, he called his dog Liebchen and made it sit up for little pieces of raw steak. How easy it is to invent a humanity, for anyone at all. What an available temptation.

In this quotation, from Chapter 24, Offred remembers a documentary that she watched about a woman who was the mistress of a Nazi death camp guard. She recalls how the woman insisted that her lover was not a "monster," and she compares that woman's situation to her own, as she spends her evenings with the Commander and comes to almost like him. The Commander seems like a good person: he is kind, friendly, genial, and even courtly to Offred. Yet he is also the agent of her oppression—both directly, as her Commander, and indirectly, through his role in constructing the oppressive edifice of Gileadean society. Like the concentration camp guard, he is "not a monster, to her"; yet he is still a monster. Offred suggests that it is "easy," when you know an evil person on a personal level, to "invent a humanity" for them. It is a "temptation," she says, meaning that no one wants to believe that someone they know is a monster. But in the case of the Commander, that temptation must be resisted. He may be kind and gentle, but he still bears responsibility for the evil of Gilead.

5. The problem wasn't only with the women, he says.
    The main problem was with the men. There was
    nothing for them anymore . . . I'm not talking about
    sex, he says. That was part of it, the sex was too
    easy . . . You know what they were complaining
    about the most? Inability to feel. Men were turning off
    on sex, even. They were turning off on marriage. Do
    they feel now? I say. Yes, he says, looking at me.
    They do.

This quotation, from the end of Chapter 32, recounts the Commander's attempt to explain to Offred the reasons behind the foundation of Gilead. His comments are ambiguous, perhaps deliberately so, but they are the closest thing to a justification for the horror of Gilead that any character offers. He suggests that feminism and the sexual revolution left men without a purpose in life. With their former roles as women's protectors taken away, and with women suddenly behaving as equals, men were set adrift. At the same time, changing sexual mores meant that sex became so easy to obtain that it lost meaning, creating what the Commander calls an "inability to feel." By making themselves soldiers, providers, and caretakers of society again, men have meaning restored to their lives. This sounds almost noble, except that in order to give meaning to men's lives, both men and women have lost all freedom. The benefits of the new world are not worth the cost in human misery.

QUOTATIONS

KEY FACTS

FULL TITLE
The Handmaid's Tale

AUTHOR
Margaret Atwood

TYPE OF WORK
Novel

GENRE
Anti-utopian (or "dystopian") novel; science fiction; feminist
political novel

LANGUAGE
English

TIME AND PLACE WRITTEN
Early 1980s, West Berlin and Alabama

DATE OF FIRST PUBLICATION
1986

PUBLISHER
McClelland & Stewart in Canada, Houghton Mifflin in the
United States

NARRATOR
Offred, a Handmaid in the Republic of Gilead

POINT OF VIEW
The Handmaid's Tale is told from Offred's point of view. She
tells the story in the immediate present tense but frequently
shifts to past tense for flashbacks to life before Gilead and to her
time in the Red Center. Much of her narration is concerned not
with events or action, but with her emotional state, which is
often affected by the memories that well up from her
happier past.

TONE
The novel's tone is dark, and at times elegiac for the lost world
before Gilead. Consistently unhappy, Offred finds both refuge
and pain in her memories. A sense of fear and paranoia also

pervades the novel, since all the characters live under a ruthless, totalitarian government.

TENSE

Offred describes her life in the Commander's home in the present tense but frequently shifts to the past tense to describe flashbacks and memories.

SETTING (TIME)

The not-too-distant future

SETTING (PLACE)

Cambridge, Massachusetts

PROTAGONIST

Offred

MAJOR CONFLICT

The Republic of Gilead has subjugated women and reduced Handmaids like Offred to sexual slavery. Offred desires happiness and freedom, and finds herself struggling against the totalitarian restrictions of her society.

RISING ACTION

Offred's evenings with the Commander; her shopping trips with Ofglen; her visit to Jezebel's

CLIMAX

After learning that Ofglen committed suicide to avoid arrest, Offred returns home and Serena confronts her about her trip to Jezebel's.

FALLING ACTION

Offred's arrest or escape at the end of the novel

THEMES

Women's bodies as political instruments; language as a tool of power; the causes of complacency

MOTIFS

Rape and sexual violence; religious terms used for political purposes; similarities between reactionary and feminist ideologies

KEY FACTS

SYMBOLS
Cambridge, Massachusetts; Harvard University; the
Handmaids' red habits; a palimpsest; the Eyes

FORESHADOWING
Offred's kiss with Nick foreshadows their eventual affair; the
attempted kidnapping of Offred's daughter foreshadows
Offred's eventual loss of her child; Ofglen's arrest foreshadows
Offred's own arrest.

KEY FACTS

Study Questions & Essay Topics

Study Questions

1. *How does* The Handmaid's Tale *depict the intersection between politics and sexual reproduction? How is Gilead's political order defined by this intersection, and how does it affect the lives of women?*

At first, religion seems to be the central element of Gileadean society, defining all aspects of life. But, in fact, the entire structure of Gilead, including its state religion, is built around one goal: the control of reproduction. Gilead is a society facing a crisis of dramatically dropping birthrates; to solve the problem, it imposes state control on the means of reproduction—namely, the bodies of women. Controlling women's bodies can succeed only by controlling the women themselves, so Gilead's political order requires the subjugation of women. They strip women of the right to vote, the right to hold property or jobs, and the right to read.

Women are a "national resource," Gilead likes to say, but they really mean that women's ovaries and wombs are national resources. Women cease to be treated as individuals, with independent selves. Rather, they are seen potential mothers. Women internalize this state-created attitude, even independent women like Offred. At one point, lying a in a bathtub and looking at her naked form, Offred tells us that, before Gilead, she thought of her body as a tool of her desires, something that could run and jump and carry things. As a Handmaid, however, she thinks of her body as a cloud, surrounding a womb that is far more "real," than she herself is. Offred's comments show that even strong women come to see themselves as the state sees them, as prospective carriers of a new generation of Gileadeans.

2. *Discuss the significance of setting in* The Handmaid's Tale. *Why does Atwood choose to set the novel where she does?*

A number of geographic clues identify Offred's town as the former Cambridge, Massachusetts. The religiously intolerant Puritan settlers of the seventeenth century made their home in Cambridge and Massachusetts. The choice of Cambridge as a setting enables Atwood to draw a parallel between the religious intolerance and misogyny of the seventeenth century and that of the late-twentieth-century Gileadeans.

The choice of Cambridge as a setting is also significant because Cambridge is the location of Harvard University, one of America's most famous institutions of higher learning. Under Gilead's rule, Harvard Yard and its buildings have been transformed into a detention center run by the Eyes, Gilead's secret police. Bodies of executed dissidents hang from the Wall that runs around the college, and "Salvagings" (mass executions) take place in Harvard Yard, on the steps of the university's Widener Library. The setting emphasizes the way Gilead has overturned the ideals embodied by an institution of learning, such as the free pursuit of knowledge and truth, and has literally enshrined in its place a regime of lies, oppression, torture, and the denial of every American ideal.

3. *How does Gilead create and use a new vocabulary to buttress its totalitarian order?*

Gilead develops its own words to give the state control over the sentiments and ideas people can express. Since Gilead is a theocracy, where religion permeates every aspect of life, biblical terminology abounds. Servants are "Marthas," a reference to a character in the New Testament; the police are "Guardians of the Faith"; soldiers are "Angels"; and the Commanders are officially "Commanders of the Faithful." The stores have biblical names like Loaves and Fishes, All Flesh, and Milk and Honey, as do the automobiles—Behemoth, Whirlwind, and Chariot.

Language is also used to subjugate women. As opposed to Gildead's men, who are defined by their military rank and therefore by their profession, Gilead's women are defined only by their gender role, as Wives, daughters, Handmaids, or Marthas. Enemies of the state are described by labels that don't necessarily correspond to the truth. For instance, Gilead calls feminists "Unwomen," placing them not only outside of society but outside of the human race. Blacks are called "Children of Ham," and Jews "Sons of Jacob," biblical terms that set them apart from the rest of society. Even daily speech is tightly controlled. People must carry on conversations within the suffocating confines of officially sanctioned language. Saying the wrong thing can lead to a swift death, so people guard their tongues, thereby subordinating their power of speech to the power of the state.

SUGGESTED ESSAY TOPICS

1. Discuss the role of the Aunts and of Serena Joy in the novel. How do they relate to other women, and how does this make them fit into the hierarchy of Gilead?

2. Is the Commander a sympathetic character, a monster, or both?

3. Is Atwood's novel ultimately a feminist work of literature, or does it offer a critique of feminism?

4. What role does Moira play in the novel? How does her significance change as the story progresses?

REVIEW & RESOURCES

QUIZ

1. What do Offred and the other Handmaids call the detention center where they were kept?

   A. The Red Center
   B. The Gymnase
   C. The concentration camp
   D. The Blue Center

2. With whom does Offred do her shopping?

   A. Aunt Lydia
   B. Ofwarren
   C. Ofglen
   D. Moira

3. What is the name of the society in which Offred lives?

   A. Jezebel
   B. The Republic of Gilead
   C. Eurasia
   D. Narnia

4. Why do all the shops in Gilead have pictures instead of written signs?

   A. The entire society is illiterate
   B. Blacks in Gilead are not allowed to read
   C. Pictures are cheaper to produce
   D. Women in Gilead are not allowed to read

5.   What did Serena Joy do before the new society was formed?

    A.   She was a gospel singer and an advocate of "traditional values"

    B.   She was the president's wife

    C.   She was a prostitute

    D.   She was a noted feminist author and activist

6.   What function do Handmaids serve?

    A.   They wait on tables in restaurants

    B.   They clean and cook in homes

    C.   They bear children for Gilead's powerful men

    D.   They raise the children of Gilead

7.   Why is the need for Handmaids so great in Gilead?

    A.   There is a great labor shortage

    B.   There is a severe infertility problem

    C.   There are very few women left alive

    D.   Most of the men have died in the war

8.   What is the title of the man with whom Offred must have sex?

    A.   The Harem Master

    B.   The Patriarch

    C.   The Captain

    D.   The Commander

9.   Who is Luke?

    A.   Offred's husband

    B.   Offred's Commander

    C.   An Eye

    D.   Offred's son

10.   Where does *The Handmaid's Tale* take place?

    A.   Moscow

    B.   Los Angeles

    C.   Cambridge, Massachusetts

    D.   Savannah, Georgia

REVIEW & RESOURCES

11. What happened to Offred's daughter?

   A. She died as an infant
   B. She was taken from Offred after she and her family
       tried to escape from Gilead
   C. She became a Handmaid
   D. She married Nick

12. What does the Commander ask Offred to do when he calls
     her into his study?

   A. Have kinky sex
   B. Strip and dance for him
   C. Tell him about her family
   D. Play Scrabble

13. What is the Wall?

   A. A place in town where bodies of executed dissidents
       are displayed
   B. A structure built along the border between Canada
       and Gilead
   C. A fence around the Commander's house to keep
       Offred in
   D. A famous structure in China

14. What does Ofglen tell Offred when they are looking at the
     prayer machines?

   A. That she is going to hell
   B. That they need to escape
   C. That Ofglen is part of a group of subversives
   D. That they should try to kill the Commander

15. Who is Moira?

   A. Offred's mother
   B. Offred's best friend
   C. Offred's daughter
   D. A Wife

16. What is the Ceremony?

    A. The ritual in which Wives and Commanders are married

    B. The execution of political dissidents

    C. A visit to church

    D. Scripture reading followed by sex between the Commander and his Handmaid

17. What is a Martha?

    A. The daughter of a Wife

    B. A female domestic servant

    C. A female soldier

    D. A kind of car in Gilead

18. How did the founders of the Republic of Gilead first clamp down on women's rights?

    A. By executing all divorced women

    B. By banning marriage and turning women into property

    C. By cutting off women's bank accounts and firing them from their jobs

    D. By making it illegal to raise daughters and taking all female children off to camps

19. What is the name of the club where the Commander takes Offred?

    A. Jezebel's

    B. The Carnival

    C. The Whorehouse

    D. All Flesh

20. Who does Offred see at the club?

    A. Aunt Lydia

    B. Her mother

    C. Her daughter

    D. Moira

21. How does Serena plan to get Offred pregnant?

    A. By having her sleep with a doctor
    B. By artificial insemination
    C. She doesn't
    D. By having her sleep with Nick

22. What is a Salvaging?

    A. A prayer meeting
    B. A mass execution
    C. A wedding
    D. A fishing expedition

23. What is the password for Ofglen's dissident group?

    A. Freedom
    B. Peace Out
    C. Mayday
    D. Hosanna

24. What happens to Ofglen?

    A. She hangs herself when she is about to be arrested
    B. She escapes from Gilead into Canada
    C. She kills her Commander and is executed
    D. She has a child

25. At the end of the novel, who comes to take Offred away?

    A. A group of Marthas
    B. The Commander's personal bodyguard
    C. A group of Aunts, who may be Eyes
    D. A pair of Eyes, who may be members of the resistance

ANSWER KEY:

1: A; 2: C; 3: B; 4: D; 5: A; 6: C; 7: B; 8: D; 9: A; 10: C;
11: B; 12: D; 13: A; 14: C; 15: B; 16: D; 17: B; 18: C; 19: A;
20: D; 21: D; 22: B; 23: C; 24: A; 25: D

A Glossary of Terms Used in *The Handmaid's Tale*

Titles

Handmaid A fertile woman who is assigned to a Commander for the purpose of bearing his children

Commander A male member of the Gileadean elite

Wife A female member of the Gileadean elite who is married to a Commander

Martha A female domestic servant

Guardian Male Gileadeans too young, old, or physically weak for the army. Guardians serve as a police force and often work for the Commanders as servants.

Angel A member of the Gileadean military

Aunt An older, unmarried woman. The Aunts serve as disciplinarians and midwives, and indoctrinate future Handmaids with Gileadean ideology.

Eye A member of the Gileadean secret police

Econowife The wife of a poor Gileadean

OTHER TERMS

Salvaging A public execution

Prayvaganza A public gathering, either of women or men. Female prayvaganzas are usually weddings for the Wives' daughters; male prayvaganzas celebrate military victories

Particicution An execution carried out by a large group of people

Birth Day The day when a Handmaid goes into labor and delivers a child

Unbaby A baby born malformed or otherwise defective, and so discarded

Unwoman A term applied to feminists and other female enemies of the state

Gender traitors Homosexuals

Children of Ham A term derived from the Bible, used to refer to African Americans

Sons of Jacob Jews

SUGGESTIONS FOR FURTHER READING

BRISCOE, LEE THOMPSON. *Scarlet Letters: Margaret Atwood's* THE HANDMAID'S TALE. Toronto: ECW Press, 1997.

INGERSOLL, EARL G., ed. *Margaret Atwood: Conversations.* Princeton, New Jersey: Ontario Review Press, 1990.

MCCOMBS, JUDITH, ed. *Critical Essays on Margaret Atwood.* Boston: G. K. Hall & Co., 1988.

RAO, ELEONORA. *Strategies for Identity: The Fiction of Margaret Atwood.* New York: Peter Lang Publishing, 1994.

STAELS, HILDA. *Margaret Atwood's Novels: A Study of Narrative Discourse.* Tubingen, Germany: Francke Verlag, 1995.

WILSON, SHARON ROSE. *Margaret Atwood's Fairy-Tale Sexual Politics.* Jackson: University Press of Mississippi, 1993.

REVIEW & RESOURCES

SPARKNOTES
TEST PREPARATION
GUIDES

The SparkNotes team figured it was time to cut standardized tests down to size. We've studied the tests for you, so that SparkNotes test prep guides are:

Smarter:
Packed with critical-thinking skills and test-
taking strategies that will improve your score.

Better:
Fully up to date, covering all new features of the tests,
with study tips on every type of question.

Faster:
Our books cover exactly what you need to
know for the test. No more, no less.

SparkNotes Study Guides: